BABY SLEEP TRAINING

The Complete Baby Sleep Guide for Modern Parents, Effective Techniques to Help Your Baby Get a Good Night's Sleep.

Daniel Rott

The following Book is reproduced below with the goal of providing information that is as accurate and reliable as possible. Regardless, purchasing this Book can be seen as consent to the fact that both the publisher and the author of this book are in no way experts on the topics discussed within and that any recommendations or suggestions that are made herein are for entertainment purposes only. Professionals should be consulted as needed prior to undertaking any of the action endorsed herein.

This declaration is deemed fair and valid by both the American Bar Association and the Committee of Publishers Association and is legally binding throughout the United States.

Furthermore, the transmission, duplication or reproduction of any of the following work including specific information will be considered an illegal act irrespective of if it is done electronically or in print. This extends to creating a secondary or tertiary copy of the work or a recorded copy and is only allowed with an expressed written consent from the Publisher.

All additional rights reserved.

The information in the following pages is broadly considered to be a truthful and accurate account of facts, and as such any inattention, use or misuse of the information in question by the reader will render any resulting actions solely under their purview. There are no scenarios in which the publisher or the original author of this work can be in any fashion deemed liable for any hardship or damages that may befall them after undertaking information described herein.

Additionally, the information in the following pages is intended only for informational purposes and should thus be thought of as universal.

As befitting its nature, it is presented without assurance regarding its prolonged validity or interim quality. Trademarks that are mentioned are done without written consent and can in no way be considered an endorsement from the trademark holder.

Contents

Introduction

Are you finding it tough to make your baby sleep throughout the night? So she wakes up quite frequently in between, and leaves you puzzled and perplexed?

Well, you are not alone.

This is the common scenario with the new parents wherein they are not sure how to train their babies to sleep throughout the night properly. Undoubtedly, your baby is still getting familiar with the day and night concept of the world and is slowly making its way.

In such a case, all you need to do is stay patient, and support her throughout. Understand her needs and guide her slowly. We will help you out.

In this guide, we will walk you through various ways in which you can guide your baby to sleep peacefully throughout the night.

Let's get started.

Signs That Your Baby Is Not Getting Enough Sleep

How to tell if the baby is sleep deprived or not. According to researchers, there are certain signs which will help you know if your baby is not getting enough sleep. Some of these signs which need to look for are

- Baby is yawning very frequently and rubbing their eyes

Yawning and eye rubbing is a universal indication of your body being discharged and holds for nearly all age groups. Kids tend to yawn and continuously rub their eyes when sleep is calling them. A new-born baby needs about 16 to 18 hours of sleep in a day. If she is not getting this much sleep, you need to make changes in her daily routine. Not getting enough sleep may make them overly tired too.

- Your baby is constantly throwing tantrums and is fussy

If your baby is sleep-deprived, she will tend to be more fussy, cranky, and sulky altogether. Even after waking up from sleep, she isn't cheerful or happy; she is either hungry or is still devoid of sleep. If she is not hungry and still fussy, it's probable, and she didn't complete her sleep well.

- Baby sleeps during short car rides and while on walks in a
  stroller

If your baby gets in deep sleep even during short car rides and while you are strolling her in a pram, she is probably overly tired and getting insufficient sleep.

- When your baby is groggy after waking up from sleep

This is another sign of your baby being sleep deprived. If she is groggy for a while even after waking from sleep, she probably needs it more. Don't try to wake her up in such situations and let her sleep enough. This usually happens when they woke up prematurely or didn't get restful sleep due to an unfamiliar environment.

- When a baby is snoring without being sick

It's normal for babies to snore in the early period of their life when their airwaves are maturing or when they occasionally catch a cold. However, if they are doing it frequently it's one of the signs of some sleep disorder. This could mean that your baby is not able to breathe properly while sleeping, which is interfering with her sound sleep. If she wakes up prematurely and snores while sleeping, consulting a doctor will be good to eliminate your worries.

- When your baby is hyperactive

If your baby is hyperactive or high on activity, means she devotes most of her time playing, which makes her too tired to get enough sleep. Such babies don't fall asleep frequently, which makes them sleep-deprived. With such kids, you need to make sure to get them to bed on time even if they are unwilling to.

- When your baby is crying too much

If your baby is crying, this doesn't always imply that your baby is sleep-deprived, however, if she is crying for no particular reason and is crying more often, the possibility is she showing signs of being tired and sleepy.

- When the baby is unwilling to face you

A baby turns away when she is making herself fall asleep by not facing things that could keep her awake such as looking at her toys or towards her father or such. If she is doing so at unusual hours and out of her usual traits, she is willing to seek more sleep because of being sleep deprived. If your baby is doing so, pay attention to the signs and lull her to a peaceful sleep.

- Baby is touching her face more often

Every kid has her way of doing things which her mother knows well. Most babies rub their eyes, touch their eyes, ears, and nose to make thyself fall asleep. If your baby is doing that more often, it simply implies that she is overly tired and needs sleep ASAP.

- Your baby becomes extra clingy

When your baby is extra clingy during unusual hours and starts to cry as you keep her down, it is a sign she wants to sleep and is seeking a comfortable place to cuddle and sleep. So if your baby is over clingy, take out your time to lull her to sleep.

- The baby is refusing to eat properly

When your baby is not eating properly and has become a fussy eater makes them fall asleep late at night and usually wakes up in the middle of the night too. This disturbs their sleeping pattern and ends up making them feel overtired than usual during the daytime. If your baby is fussing overeating too, it is a sign that she is not getting enough sleep.

- The baby wakes up late in the morning

Kids who have slept well during the night will naturally wake up in the morning at their routine time or even early. They woke up easily with the slightest of stimulations like through falling sunlight on your face or being called up my mother. However, when the kid is overtired, she tends to keep sleeping and it is difficult to wake them up from their slumber. Even after waking up, they would still not be fully awake. This is one of the signs of her not getting enough sleep.

- Your baby is not talkative during the day

When your baby is showing unusual behavior during the daytime and is not talking much or not seeking much attention, it is one of the signs that she is tired and sleep-deprived. She wants to get some sleep as she can.

These were some of the common signs that can make you proactive if your baby is not getting enough sleep.

Factors That Might Impact Your Baby's Sleep

Sleep is one of the most fundamental necessities for human beings to survive. It's more important than food. An average person can stay alive for about three weeks without food, but without proper sleep, you may not be able to last even a week, with the longest recorded instance without sleep is 11 consecutive days.

When it comes to sleep, it seems like babies need it more than we, adults. 6-8 hours of sleep is generally advised for adults, but that number goes up to 14 to 17 hours for infants, 11 to 14 hours for babies, and at least 10 hours for preschoolers.

Importance of Sleep for Babies

It is estimated that babies will spend 40% of their childhood sleeping. This is important both for their mental and physical development. There are mainly two types of sleep, Non-rapid eye movement (NREM) and Rapid eye movement (REM).

In NREM, our sleep is quiet, and the body is inactive. Energy restoration and cell and tissue repair occur during this phase. In REM, our brain is active, and we enter the dream phase. Both of these are important. Babies spend 50% of their sleeping time in both REM and NREM. The sleep cycle in each one of them is 50 minutes.

When they sleep, it improves their learning ability. Studies have continuously shown that = efficient sleep time is good for babies and their cognition. Quality sleep also impacts their growth.

Finally, babies sleep peacefully, enjoy a better mood with easier temperament. They become easy to handle and more approachable. This makes your life, as a parent, easier too.

What Can Break Your Baby's Good Night Sleep?

More and more parents are complaining about their babies being irritable and hard to handle when they're awake. While there can be dozens of reasons for this, one of them can be lack of quality sleep which you shouldn't overlook. With their sleep cycles typically being 50 minutes in each cycle, babies tend to wake up in the middle of the night, disrupting your sleep in the process.

Here are some of the factors that impact their sleep:

- Noise

Babies are very responsive to noise, and if the sound is just enough to reach them, then this can break their sleep. Disruptive household noises like noise from the living room, kitchen, closing and opening of doors, doorbells, and cell phone ringtones are most likely to wake your newborn up. Even the noise coming outside of your house can cause disturbances.

Noise generated either from the household or outside of the household should be monitored. For example, in the room where the baby is sleeping or in the adjacent rooms, don't allow TVs, music system, games to be played too loud. Also, try not to socialize and gather in the room and start gossiping about how your day went and what not. In doing so, you won't even realize when the decibels are going up, and in the end, you'll wake up your baby. While monitoring outside noises may not be possible, you can certainly try to minimize them or close all the doors and windows to block the sound.

- Temperature change

Temperature can hugely impact your baby's sleep. They usually prefer a cool temperature during warm weather and warmer temperature during cold weather. A blanket or comforters is usually desired by toddlers, which makes them feel safe. In hot temperature, make sure to maintain a consistently cool temperature by either air conditioning, cooler, or fan. If you're only using a fan, make sure the ventilation of the room is sufficient to keep the temperature cool.

With a lack of ventilation, the room often gets warmer, which can irritate the baby. Conversely, if the weather is cold, make sure the room is warm with arrangement for blankets, socks, and muffler. To avoid your baby from waking up in the middle of the night, try to keep the temperature consistent.

- The lighting of the room

Most babies fall asleep irrespective of lighting conditions. They're more inclined to those swaying and patting. But it's better to keep a dark, dim environment which will help them fall asleep more easily.

Once it learns that a dark environment is a sign to get some sleep, he/she will get accustomed to the sleep-inducing atmosphere and fall asleep easily as soon as you dim the lights. When in sleep mode, it's crucial that you maintain that lighting level. However, it's not advised to completely darken the room since if your child wakes up in the middle of the night, she will not be able to see anything and get frightened.

- Interrupted bedtime routine

A bedtime routine allows your baby to calm down and develop the feeling of sleepiness before ultimately dozing off. Just like adults, a bedtime routine will unwind her from her day as it is difficult to fall asleep immediately after a busy day. So it's good to develop a bedtime ritual which serves as a clue to the baby that it's time to sleep. Most fundamental bedtime routine tasks are dealing with separation and identifying problem spots.

Bedtime can get scary for your little one. This is because she gets separated from the people (or the parents) that she loves the most. Dealing with it initially will be a huge challenge for the baby, but once she gets accustomed to it, falling asleep will get much easier. Every child has a problem falling off. A bedtime routine focuses on finding and correcting that.

Once you've developed a fitting bedtime routine, it's better to stick with it till she gets older. An interruption or changes to it might pose problems to your child's sleep.

- Change in person

Babies get accustomed to a specific person (usually either the mother or father) who regularly puts them to bed. If this person is changed by a nanny or other family member, then they may face trouble sleeping. This is part of the "bedtime routine" discussed above. If they wake up in the middle of the night and don't find that person, they may not go to sleep again.

- Hunger

The feeling of hunger is really displeasing to your baby, just like adults. But adults can better cope with the feeling, but babies cannot. If they feel the signs of hunger, they'll get desperate and either won't be able to sleep or wake up in the middle of the night.

They will let you know that they're hungry by either crying, acting restless, sucking on fist, going for your breast, etc. You just have to feed the baby at that time, and everything should be back to normal. They generally demand food every 2 to 3 hours. It's also important to feed her well before she goes to bed to avoid mid-night hunger.

- Wet diaper

The condition of the diapers affects your child's sleep to a greater degree. A dry and warm diaper is preferred by the baby, while a wet diaper can annoy her. Moreover, a wet diaper can cause rashes and irritations, which you obviously won't want as a parent. Before putting your baby to sleep, it's best to use a disposable diaper instead of a cloth diaper. Cloth diapers aren't able to soak up moisture while disposable diapers can handle that. Also if you're clothing them up, then go for loose pajamas which allows you easy access to the diapers.

- Circadian rhythm

A circadian rhythm is a 24-hour clock inside our body that regulates our sleep and wakefulness period. While it does not apply to babies less than six months old, babies older than six months get used to a certain rhythm during which they sleep and wake up. Bedtime routine aids in the development of this biological rhythm.

But the most influencing factor is light. Therefore, it is advised to dim the lights while to try to put your baby to sleep. After six months, she gets used to this cycle and finds it easy to doze off. On the other hand, changes made to it might make it difficult for her.

- Genetics

Even though the theory is recently confined, genes do play a role in how your baby sleeps through the night. Researchers at Quebec, Canada, studied sleep of almost 1000 identical and fraternal twins and found out that genes influence how the baby sleeps at night.

But in the study, the genes that affected sleep weren't taken into consideration, rather it was a study to find whether identical twins shared sleep patterns more than fraternal twins -- and the results were positive. They did share some sleeping patterns.

- Medical complication

Some babies suffer from medical complications, which affect their sleep. One such condition is "Infant Sleep Apnea." It is a sleep-related breathing disorder which causes a reduction in breathing while the baby is asleep. As a result, she wakes up in the night.

It's important that parents don't let leave this unchecked, which can become life-threatening. It is one of the main causes of Sudden Infant Death Syndrome (SIDS) which occurs in babies under one year of age. Also, you should protect her from any infections which can hinder her health and sleep.

Month By Month Babies Sleep Pattern

A baby, while going through many developmental milestones, will also adapt to different sleep schedules in the first few months. This transition is never easy, and as most new parents know, their sleep will have to be sacrificed at certain times.

But that is a part of bringing up a child, and as a parent, you will sign up for the exhaustion willingly. This, however, does not continue because your baby will settle into a pattern as the month's pass, and you will be able to induce some healthy sleeping habits along the way.

Now, since the sleeping schedules will be rather unpredictable in the first few months, it is important to make sure that the baby is getting the right amount of sleep. The best way to ensure this is by making sure that your baby is not overstimulated.

Overstimulation in babies might occur due to environmental conditions or physiological factors. Therefore, it is important to make sure that nothing stresses or causes anxiety. Most of the time, if your baby is well-fed and comforted, then she will not be overstimulated and will be able to fall asleep easily.

Given below is the usual sleeping schedule observed in babies during the first twelve months. This will help new parents to have an idea about what to expect and how to maintain sound sleeping habits.

Sleep Survival (first month)

Your newborn's sleep pattern will seem irregular at this stage. This is completely normal, and there is no cause for worry. Your baby will sleep throughout the day and will only wake up when she is hungry.

At this time, babies are unable to stay awake for more than forty minutes, and sometimes they need to be woken up, to get cleaned, to be fed or change clothes. This is the period during which a baby should get maximum sleep, and the conditions around should not be stressful in any way.

Do not give your baby any sleeping aids or wake her up unnecessary. Also, as a new parent, this phase will be exhausting, even if your baby is sleeping most of the time. Therefore, it is essential that you get enough rest, as well.

Sleep Learning (second and third months)

During these months, babies start adjusting into some schedule. They can stay awake longer than usual, and as the gaps between naps increase, they can focus on other activities, developing motor and cognitive skills. However, they are not able to stay awake for more than a couple of hours at a time.

It is important that you fit in a full feeding schedule, based on these gaps, as for them these two hours are a significant change from staying awake for forty minutes. This is also the period during which parents should be introducing healthy sleeping habits and patterns. A proper night time sleeping schedule, following a full meal, is a good pattern to induce at this stage. Past the two hour mark, your baby will become overstimulated or overtired, and you do not want that to happen.

Therefore, try to understand the sleeping cues and identify when your baby needs to sleep. This will help avoid unnecessary stress.

Establishing and Maintaining Sound Sleeping Habits (fourth, fifth and sixth months)

These three months will see significant changes in the sleeping patterns of a baby. However, patterns will differ from one new-born to another. For example, some babies might already be sleeping twice during the day, while others might still be taking frequent naps. Some might also sleep through the entire night. This period is also the time during which some babies experience sleep regression.

The 4-month sleep regression is very common and during it, your baby will wake up, especially at night and then refuse to go to sleep at all. As these three months will be seeing some transitions in terms of sleep patterns, several changes in habits, like not swaddling your baby anymore or sleeping in a crib instead of the baby bassinet, can also be introduced.

At night, even if your baby is not experiencing sleep regression, it is important to feed her once and during the day, she needs to be fed at least five times.

Having Consistent, And Healthy Sleeping Habits (from the sixth month till the tenth month)

In these few months, a proper routine can be introduced, and the baby will start to follow it. Some babies might not sleep through the night even now. However, this is a great time to start implementing a schedule which will help your baby to have a better sleeping pattern. For many babies, sleeping cues will now be consistent and very easy to identify. This will help in establishing the routine.

During this time, babies, when put down in their cot, will try to sleep on their own. To further this progress, it is important that you put your baby down when she is still drowsy but not fully asleep. This will allow for some practice to sleep on their own without any associations, like having to be swaddled, or rocked or held and cuddled.

Avoiding Sleep Regression or Any Setbacks (from the tenth month to the twelfth month)

By this time your baby will already have a sleeping pattern and will probably be sleeping through the night. However, after the fourth month, sleep regressions may occur when your baby is eight, nine, or ten months. This will disrupt all sleeping patterns and be stressful for your baby and thus needs to be avoided.

Sleep regressions at this age occur when there is some change in the surroundings which make the baby uncomfortable, and parents must remember to not introduce or subject their baby to any sudden changes. That might cause anxiety and affect sleep schedule. Now, certain setbacks might occur where you will notice that your baby is sleeping very less and is not even napping during the daytime.

It is very important to comfort your baby at this time and look for cues to figure out what might be causing these setbacks. Above all, your baby will need to be in a safe and healthy environment to encourage the development of body and mind. If that is done, then automatically of the sleep schedule will be maintained without any setbacks.

Why Do Babies Cry In Sleep?

After a long, hectic day, you put your baby to rest in her crib and go to sleep, only to find that she has woken up at 2 am and is demanding immediate regard. One of the worst nightmares parents face when raising their toddlers is them crying in the middle of the night. So what's possibly going wrong in there?

They Wake up Every Two to Four Hours

Even though toddlers sleep for an average of about 16 to 20 hours per day, they wake up every two to four hours in their sleep time. This is applicable for both day sleep and night sleep hours. Unlike adults who have a longer sleep cycle, babies have a shorter sleep cycle which continuously keeps developing during their growth phase. They spend about 50 minutes each in the REM (Rapid eye movement) and NREM phase roughly, but generally more time in REM phase. When this cycle ends, they can wake up from their sleep.

However, not all crying signs are similar. On average, a baby can wake up <u>4 to 5 times per night</u>. These awakenings are brief, and most babies can put themselves back to sleep without requiring attention. They're just transitioning from one sleep phase to another. So it's important that you don't wake her up completely and start feeding her or change diapers.

Babies after 4 to 6 months will become capable of sleeping 8 to 12 hours straight if left undisturbed. Some require more than six months to develop this habit. Even though that's a <u>claim</u>, it can only be true if the factors following this point don't come into play.

Hunger and Thirst

Just like a toddler won't be able to put herself to sleep if she's hungry, the chances are that she might get up and start crying if she feels the same during her sleep. Most parents think that if their baby is not crying, then she is sleeping. But that's not the case. As their sleeping cycle is shorter, they can remain awake and still be silent. After a few minutes, they put themselves back to sleep.

Babies feeding cycle is small, too, and they tend to eat every three to four hours. During those brief night waking period, if they experience hunger or thirst sensation, then definitely they'll cry for help. But knowing whether or not your child is hungry is a tough ask. Sometimes, it might be for other reasons like needing a parent by their side to get back to sleep. So it's important to look for the cue that she generally signals when she's genuinely hungry like approaching your breast, sucking thumb, etc.

Irritation

If your baby gets irritated in some ways during her sleep, then she'll definitely cry out for help to get relieved. Irritation can be from a number of causes, but one of the most common reasons is diaper rash. It can make your baby's skin sore, itchy, and scaly. Babies lack control over their excretory functions and can poop or pee in the middle of the night.

That's why it is recommended to use disposable diapers during the night time, which can retain much of the water. But still if left for too long, it rubs against your baby's skin and can irritate. This may also lead to an allergic reaction or infection, which can hinder your baby's sleep. Eczema is the medical term used to define such red bumps and sores condition.

Food allergies are another reason for irritation. If you've fed something new or any substance that didn't go down well with your baby, it can cause skin reactions, respiratory symptoms, stomach upsets, etc. Vomiting, hives, itching, or weakness is crying are some signs which indicate that the cause might be food allergies. You should seek immediate medical attention for this cause.

Lastly, irritations can be caused by insect or mosquito bites. As babies skin are tender than adults, the bites can be even more frustrating, if not painful. Therefore, make proper use of insect repellent in the room where you put your baby to sleep.

Illness

If your baby is suffering from some illness, then she might cry for help on feeling uncomfortable during the night awakening hours. If you know about the illness, then obviously you'll be ready for such situations. But if it's sudden, then you should try your best to treat your baby. A weak, moaning cry most often signals something is wrong. High temperature is another indicator.

Babies who suffer from colic can wake up and start crying continuously for several minutes. Babies mostly in their 6 to 8 weeks period suffer from this condition, but as time goes by, the condition improves on its own. While there's nothing much you can do about it, you should soothe the baby and try to get her back to sleep.

Nightmares

Whether or not babies have nightmares is still a debate with no conclusive evidence. As per baby's sleep cycle, she spends around 50 minutes or more in the REM phase. Our eyes are in rapid motion, and all of us have dreaming experiences during this phase.

Babies experience something called "Confusional Arousal" where they seem agitated and scared in their sleep, which is followed by sudden crying. But the baby is not completely awake and is still in her sleep. So parents should only try to calm their baby down and put her back to sleep gently. If this is because of nightmares or some other reason is not clear. But even if they do, they have limited memory power, so they can easily put the thoughts behind and go back to sleep with the help of a parent.

Some babies start having night terrors at the age of around 18 months, but this is highly common, because of their limited memory and experience with the outer world. Nightmares are more common in children aged 2 to 4 years. But by around that time, most of them get equipped to handle it by themselves.

How Your Parental Practices Affect Baby's Sleep

According to a study conducted at the University of Montreal, researchers stated that how parents put their babies to sleep has a direct impact on how the baby sleeps through the night.

The study involved 987 moms and dads who were asked some questions regarding their parental practices, how they help their child sleep, psychological qualities, and socio-demographic data of babies.

Then they recorded the sleep habits of babies, total sleep hours, and difficulties babies face to fall asleep. They found that parental behaviors that affected their baby's sleep the most are:

- Parents who fed their babies within a few minutes after they're awoke provoked bad dreams, delays in sleep, and less than ten hours of sleep.
- Co-sleeping delayed sleeping back for babies by as much as 15 minutes.

When babies wake up in the middle of the night and begin to cry, mothers think that they're hungry and start feeding her. But doing so causes bad dreams and delay in falling back to sleep. Co-sleeping with babies isn't a good option either.

Night Feeding and Night Weaning: When and How

At about six months of age, you will begin to see some significant development in your baby. Now, if you are still breastfeeding your baby, then this is a good time to start weaning and especially night weaning.

But, if you are feeding your baby from a bottle, then you might want to consider phasing out the night feeds. However, babies are usually not hungry at night as they consume enough during the day to stay healthy.

Still, you can decide if you want to introduce night feeding and observe your baby's feeding patterns and habits to figure out how to phase out the night feeds. Now, phasing out night feeds is not something that you need to rush into, but rather you should concentrate on creating a sound feeding schedule for your baby.

Usually, mothers prefer to keep breastfeeding their babies at night because this allows the milk flow to remain uninterrupted. But, even if they only breastfeed their babies during the day, the milk flow will not stop. It is important to keep this in mind if you are going to consider night weaning.

Night weaning should ideally be started when your baby is about four to six months old. After which, to regulate sleep patterns, you will have to gradually phase out the night feeds. This will allow your baby to sleep through the night, without needing to be fed at any time during the night.

Night Feeding At Different Ages

Night feeding patterns cannot remain constant because they prevent your baby from sleeping through the entire night. To ensure that your baby gets adequate sleep, you will have to change the number of times that you are feeding your baby at night and then slowly begin to phase out the night feeds.

Given below are the number of times that you should feed your baby at night, depending upon your baby's age.

- New-born to three months

When your baby is a new-born, and till about three months of age, you will need to feed your baby every two to three hours. At this age, babies sleep almost all the time and have no concept of day or night. So, they will wake from time to time, demanding to be fed.

- Three to four months

At this age, your baby should slowly be introduced to the differences between day and night. At night, your baby will not wake up very frequently but might be able to sleep for about six hours at a stretch, after which you will have to feed her.

However, this is a rather ideal situation, and often babies are not able to sleep for that long. Therefore, during this period, you will have to feed your baby twice or thrice during the night.

- Five to six months

Night feedings should become even less frequent during this time. You should not feed your baby more than two times during the night at this age.

- Seven to nine months

This is the time to start weaning your baby from night feedings (if you haven't begun the process already). One feeding should be enough at this age, but sometimes, you can allow two feedings.

- Ten to twelve months

You can feed your baby once, but only if she is demanding it and will settle at nothing else. However, be careful so that you do not reinitiate the habit of night feeding once again.

- After twelve months

No night feedings are necessary at this age. Your baby will already be sleeping through the night by the time she is a year old, so you do not need to worry. But, if a particularly stressful situation arises, resort to different techniques to soothe your baby, instead of trying to feed her as that no longer is the right solution.

How Should You Feed Your Baby At Night?

Night feeding is not very easy. No matter how old your baby is, you have to keep in mind that the slightest excitement will disrupt her sleeping schedule. If your baby is a new-born, then as mentioned before, she will not have the concept of day and night.

However, it is important to slowly help her differentiate between the two. Now, if your baby is a few months old, then it is equally important to let her understand that night-time is for sleeping for longer hours.

Even then, your baby might continue to wake up, needing to be fed. Given below are some steps to that you can follow to make sure that your baby is not overexcited before bed, but also has a hassle-free night feeding.

- Do not wake your baby up to feed her

If your baby does not wake on her own, then wait. Babies usually sleep for two to three hours before waking up, and you do not need to wake them up yourself. Sometimes newborns sleep for about five hours before they wake because they are already getting enough nutrition when you feed them during the day.

But if you find that your baby is underweight, then you should wake her up (but only after having a doctor to confirm the weight issues), a couple of times during the night, to feed them.

- Once you have fed your baby, make sure to burp her

Babies who are not burped get very uncomfortable, due to the air trapped in the stomach, and this will cause quite some stress. If you do not burp your baby, then she will not be able to get back to sleep and will become very restless, often leading to tears.

- Make sure your baby is sleeping near you

Keeping your baby's cot near your bed will get you to stay alert. This way, when your baby wakes up, you will be able to immediately attend her, as is especially important for babies who need to be fed at night.

Keep all the supplies like water bottle, feeding bottle (if you are not breastfeeding your baby) in the room itself. This will help you stay organized. If you allow too much time to pass, once your baby wakes up, she might become quite frantic.

- When you feed your baby at night, do not immediately turn on any bright lights.

Remember, while night feeding, you are also helping your baby to understand the difference between day and night. This can be done by introducing different intensities of light, during different times. Also, while night feeding, if you turn on a very bright light, that will hold your baby's attention, and you will not be able to feed her properly.

After a night feed, do not immediately cuddle or hold your baby. Allow your baby to settle down, and you can sing a lullaby or stroke her head gently. This way, babies learn to soothe themselves and slowly fall asleep on their own after being fed.

When Is A Baby Ready For Night Weaning?

New parents are often confused as to when they should start night weaning. Now, this is rather tricky because each baby is ready at a different age. Not all babies can be night weaned at four months, while others develop so fast, that you can begin to phase out their night feeds at six months of age.

Usually, between four to six months, babies consume enough calories during the day that should get them through the night (five to six hours of sleep). Now, often it is seen, that the younger ones (four months or less) can sleep for longer hours without waking up and needing to be fed. However, the babies who are a little older (around six months of age) wake up a couple of times during the night and have to be fed before they settle down.

Babies who are breastfed, do not only wake up during the night because they are feeling hungry. They often do so because they want to be held and cuddled. If your baby is needing this, then this might be a time that you will consider night weaning, especially if you are a working mother.

If you are away for work or not with your baby all the time, then your baby might want to be nursed more often, to feel close to you. Also, if your baby is going through some major developmental changes (like teething) or is ill, then she will wake up quite often. Therefore, you need to understand why your baby is waking up during the night and needs to be nursed before settling down to sleep again.

Once you figure that out, you can gradually introduce night weaning, keeping in mind that your baby will need a lot of comfort and reassurance all along the way, as she is still very young.

Generally, babies between four to six months of age can be weaned from their night-time feedings. At this age, you do not need to feed your baby at night because they will have had enough during the day. But, out of habit, your baby might wake up at the middle of the night, wanting to be fed. Now, some babies are used to waking up during the night and being fed immediately (which helps them settle down), and usually, this is where the habit develops. If this is the situation with your baby, then it will take some time to change the pattern.

How Should You Night Wean Your Baby?

More often than not, unnecessary night feeding is bound to disrupt your baby's sleep. If you continue night feeding for a very long time, then your baby will develop the habit of continuously waking up, and if there is no balance between these night feeds, your baby might start wetting the bed more frequently and having digestive problems. Therefore, it is important to wean your baby, and the following are some tips that will help with night weaning.

- Do not rush the weaning process.

Give your baby some time, and to do this, you can nurse your baby for a shorter period. Make sure that there is a significant interval between feedings and during this time, try settling your baby down to sleep.

- Make sure that your baby is eating well during the day.

If your baby is consuming the adequate amounts of nutrients during the day, then it is unlikely that she will wake up more than a couple of times during the night.

- Feed your baby several times in the evening.

When your baby goes to bed full, she will be able to sleep through the night most of the time.

- If your baby wakes up at night crying, then ask your partner to comfort her.

Your baby can identify your smell, and the smell of your breast milk and therefore, your presence can excite your baby and lead her to think that it is time for another feeding.

As your baby grows older, you will have to slowly stop all night feeding. If your baby does wake up in the middle of the night, soothe her, and explain that it is not the time to eat. This is usually done to babies, who are a little older and in such situations, you can explain that they can have their bottle in the morning, but they need to go back to sleep now. Similarly, do not immediately nurse your baby at such times. However, if you see that your baby is becoming frantic, and is demanding to be fed, then go back to the usual pattern. You can try again after a week or so, but do not push too much.

Ways to Make Your Baby Fall Asleep

Newborns usually have a pretty erratic sleep schedule and take time to settle into a steady routine. They sleep a lot throughout the day. However, most of the time, they do not sleep for a long time but wake in between for a period of about forty-five minutes.

At this stage, a baby cannot distinguish between day and night, and therefore, it is difficult to regulate her sleep schedule accordingly. But it is important to understand how a new-born sleep schedule is formed and what factors affect it if you want your baby to have healthy sleeping habits.

How Much Sleep Does Your Baby Need?

In all babies, sleeping patterns take time to emerge and to become consistent. During the first couple of months, your baby's primary need will be feeding and not sleeping. However, adequate sleep is of utmost importance, and during this time, your baby will sleep for about ten to fifteen hours a day, sometimes even eighteen hours.

Once your baby is about six months old, certain developmental milestones will be reached that might affect the sleep schedule. However, this is the time when a proper routine can be formed, and your baby will start sleeping for about six to seven hours at a stretch.

Now, there are a few general methods that can help new parents to establish a healthy sleeping pattern for their baby. These methods are given below.

- Do not distract or engage your baby's attention just before putting her to sleep.

If you see that your baby is drowsy, try to minimize activity. Babies often have the tendency to stay alert, and the slightest activity can make them curious and attentive. During this time, you can cuddle your baby, and even rock her to sleep but do not hold your baby's gaze.

Holding your baby's gaze might become a signal for playtime as is rather usual. Here, it is therefore important to not do anything that might excite your baby, other than comforting her and slowly allowing your baby to drift off to sleep.

- Keep a check on whether or not your baby is eating sufficiently

Sometimes babies do not eat the amount of food they need to and this can affect sleep schedule significantly. With babies who are still being breastfed, it is seen that during the day they feed for a few minutes and then there's a long gap before they want to be fed again.

Now, this is simply snacking, and your baby is hardly getting the right amount. This also happens when you wean your baby and she begins to have solid food as well. It is therefore very important to make sure that your baby is eating well because otherwise, lack of nutrition will lead them to be anxious and stressed; this is disrupting a healthy sleeping schedule.

- Lie your baby down on the bed when she is drowsy but not yet asleep

Nursing is very calming for newborns. It is thus seen that once a bay has been breastfed, she will start to feel sleepy. During other times of the day, when the baby has not been just nursed, she might give cues like rubbing the eyes constantly. If you notice this, then lay your baby down on the bed and soothe her while he/ she slowly drifts off to sleep.

Once babies grow older, this will develop the habit of drifting off to sleep on their own, once they lie down on the bed. But it is important that you do not try to force a sleeping schedule, but allow your baby to take time and adjust to falling asleep without any aid.

- Do not let your baby fall asleep while feeding

Newborns usually fall asleep while still being nursed. But if this is made into a habit, then it can become an issue. Sometimes when this happens, babies have trouble falling back asleep when they wake up during the night. This is because they think that they need to be fed in order to fall back asleep.

Here, sleeping and nursing overlap and nursing become another cue. What can be done in such cases is that the feeding times can be changed. If a baby is falling asleep while feeding, then she will need to be fed earlier. A few changes in the routine will help in maintaining a healthy schedule.

- Wait sometime before attending your baby if she is cooing or making soft sounds while sleeping

Sometimes while sleeping, a baby might make soft cooing sounds. This does not mean that the baby is fully awake. At such times, it is important that parents do not immediately try to lift or rock their baby because that might wake her.

The best thing to do is to allow your baby some time and see if she is eventually sleeping calmly again. Most of the time, babies are able to calm themselves on their own. However, if you see that your baby is unable to do so and that she is becoming more and more frantic, then do attend and comfort her.

- Use the lights to regulate your baby's sleep patterns

If you are able to strategically use the electric lights and the natural light during the daytime then you can teach your baby the concept of day and night. Your baby will learn to identify different parts of the day (and actions associated with that part like eating or sleeping) with the help of different intensities of light.

During the day if your baby is drowsy, make sure you are letting her sleep in a well-lit area. At night, dim the lights or use a night light that is soft and soothing. Sometimes, babies wake up in the middle of the night, but if this does happen then do not immediately switch on all lights. Keep the lights off or switch on a very dim lamp and try to calm her down.

Having different intensities of light will help your baby to adjust to the transition from day tonight. This will also help establish a good pattern as your baby will realize that the naps taken during the day are shorter than the longer one at night.

- Introduce a routine to adjust your baby's internal clock

Just like the use of lights, certain other external factors can also help regulate your baby's sleep. For example, you can start minimizing all kinds of noise and dim all the lights in the room sometime before the actual bedtime. This will act as an environmental cue and your baby will be able to relate to this. Every time you do it, your baby will know it is time for bed. This is particularly helpful when you are trying to get your baby to sleep through the entire night. You can also include other such cues like a warm bath before bedtime, or even sing a lullaby to help your baby to drift off.

- Make sure that your baby has an early bedtime once you introduce her to a proper schedule:

This is a very good habit and can be introduced to babies from a very early stage. When a baby is six weeks old, her body will start producing melatonin. Melatonin is a hormone that induces drowsiness. From this stage, parents can start an early bedtime schedule because babies will naturally adjust their internal clock and will begin to feel sleepy during sundown (that is when the melatonin levels rise).

However, this timing is of a broad range because it varies between 4:30 p.m. in winters and 8:30 p.m. during summers. Thus it is advisable that you introduce a bedtime around 6:30 or 7:00 p.m. which will be consistent with the different seasons.

- Allow your baby to take naps and do not force a different routine without giving time to adjust

Babies nap all the time. Newborns nap most of the time during the day, and this is healthy for them. Therefore, let your baby nap and do not worry about the fact that napping during the day will keep your baby awake at night. This does not happen, and it will take some time for your baby to sleep through the night.

Parents often try to introduce new schedules and change feeding times. Such a sudden change is not good for a baby, and if it is necessary, then it should be done gradually so that it does not cause any stress.

- Get your baby to sleep through the night

Now, the methods given above are general ones and they will help your baby to fall asleep at any age. The period between six to nine months is when your baby should be sleeping through the night. But this does not always happen.

Develop a Routine for Your Baby

To help your baby to sleep through the night, it is essential to introduce a proper routine. However, the problem lies with getting your baby to adjust to the routine. Following are some tips which involve certain bedtime activities that you can use to set a routine for your baby.

- Distinguish between the types of games that your baby is playing

Allow your baby to be more active during the day but lessen the excitement in the evening. This will help your baby to calm down before bedtime but also be tired enough from the day's activities to fall asleep easily.

- Do not change the pattern of activities

Play the same games every evening to introduce a routine. This will help your baby to identify and relate. A sudden change might excite or startle your baby and will make her uncomfortable.

- Play a favorite game right before bedtime

Make sure that is not sometimes too hectic and do it in your baby's bedroom. This way, your baby will look forward to playing, and the room will provide a safe and comforting space.

- Make your surroundings calm and peaceful during the evening

Do not have any harsh lights switched on or play any loud music. It is important that your baby stays calm as bedtime approaches.

- Prepare a sleepable environment

A sleepable environment is the one which has minimal noise, lights, and other sorts of disturbances. The room should be free of insects like mosquitoes, and the temperature should be regulated to neither be too cold nor too warm. These are all of the things that obstruct your child from inducing the feeling of sleepiness. It's equally important to maintain this ideal environment to allow your infant to maximize its sleeping hours.

Also, the crib should be comfortable and large enough to fit the child along with rails provided to protect your baby from accidental fall. Parents are encouraged not to sleep with their babies in the same room as it may influence her ability to sleep on her own.

- Develop a bedtime routine

A bedtime routine can help your baby drive itself towards the drowsiness state. When you do things regularly that leads to sleep, her brain counts them as cues or signals that it's time to sleep. Most babies start developing their "internal clock" by the time they hit three months.

Dimming the lights before bedtime is an example of a bedtime routine. The routine can be as short as 20 minutes or as long as an hour, but it's important to be consistent with it, especially in the beginning, to see positive results out of it.

While what activities to include in the bedtime routine is completely dependent upon the parents, it's useful to pick up those activities that are physically and mentally soothing. As opposed to adults who can easily doze off in tired and uncomfortable state, babies have a hard time doing that.

- Use bulbs that don't emit blue wavelengths

Total darkness is often the best and easiest way to fall asleep. If however, for some reason, you need lightings in your baby's room, then don't use bulbs with blue wavelengths. These lights are found to have a disruptive effect on our sleeping pattern, and younger children are more sensitive to it. Even white light, which contains the blue spectrum, can cause this hindrance. Therefore, it's advisable to install a blue-wavelength filter or a blue-wavelength-free bulb in your baby's room.

- Keep an account on the siesta

Babies spend the majority of their time sleeping. So the siesta (or the afternoon sleep) is common for them. But long afternoon naps can make your baby oversleep, which will affect her sleep at night.

The best way to tackle this problem is to keep your baby awake at least 6 hours from bedtime and encourage her to get involved in playing activities. Results have shown that babies who remain awake for at least that period before bedtime find it easier to fall asleep at night at the right time.

- Hold a no screen time rule before bed

The screens of most electronic devices emit blue wavelength lights, which can hinder the body's ability to fall asleep, as discussed in the previous point. They stop the release of essential chemicals from the brain that induces sleepiness.

Therefore, even though your kid enjoys watching TV and learns a lot of things from it, you should forbid her from having some screen time experience before going to bed. Ideally, there should be around 30 minutes gap between last screen time and bedtime.

- Teach your baby self-soothing

Self-soothing is the ability of babies to fall asleep without their parent's intervention. When babies learn to self-soothe themselves, they take a lot of workload off of you. Bedtime routines are one form of self-soothing, but that's not deliberate. They don't intentionally go for sleep, they follow the activities, and their brain commands them to go to sleep.

One best way to teach your baby self-soothing is by placing her in the crib and letting her fall asleep on her own, rather than you waiting the entire time for her to fall asleep before you leave. Initially, it will be difficult, but once your baby gets accustomed to it, it'll be a cakewalk.

- Feed your baby before putting her to sleep

It's natural for humans to feel drowsy after having meals. While concrete evidence doesn't yet exist that this is applicable for babies too, there's something called "dream feeding." This refers to the practice of feeding an infant in her sleep to help her sleep longer. Even though this play a modest role in determining baby's sleeping habit, it is something worth trying. For feeding purposes, breastfeeding is the best option as the baby is already acquainted with it and can perform even unconsciously.

- Night cries can be a pretense

When babies wake up in the middle of the night, most parents rush to change their diapers or feed them a hearty midnight snack. But it's normal for babies to wake up after bedtime and before sunrise.

In fact, partial awakening is way more common than most parents realize. A typical baby experiences 4-5 partial awakening per night. They wake up for a brief period and sleep back without informing their parents. They even cry when they're asleep, but that's normal too. They're just transitioning from one sleep phase to another.

- Always go for disposable diapers

Disposable diapers are the ones which absorb urine or feces. Even though these are pricier when compared to normal diapers, they'll make your baby's night sleep much more comfortable and safe. If the diapers fail to absorb the excretory materials, then it'll cause discomfort and rashes, ultimately ending up waking your baby.

- If your baby is constantly crying, get her checked for colic

Colic is a medical condition among babies where they cry for a prolonged period for no reason. Babies in the age bracket of 4 to 6 weeks suffer the most from colic. They cry for about 3 hours, and no measure of soothing or calming truly helps, but they stop crying on their own. Researchers haven't found out exactly why it happens, but claim it's natural and generally fades away after the age of 6 weeks.

Babies Often Wake Up In The Middle of the Night

If this happens, then the conditions of the room should be the same every night. The lights and sounds (if any) should be the same because if you change them, then the room will appear rather unfamiliar. This will make your baby frantic, and she will not be able to fall back asleep easily.

A bath before bedtime is a very good idea. You can put bath salts (after consulting your pediatrician) and let your baby splash about for a while in the tub. Bathing is an activity that soothes and calms almost instantly.

Reduce the Risk of SIDS While Putting Your Baby to Sleep

SIDS or sudden infant death syndrome is not uncommon. Precautions should always be taken to lower the risks. To do so, it is important to keep in mind the following points, whenever your baby takes a nap.

- Make sure that your baby is sleeping on her back.

Use a proper firm surface to put your baby to sleep. Do not allow your baby to fall asleep in car seats or similar places because your baby might get trapped and hurt.

Sometimes, babies fall asleep in their stroller. If this happens, then gently lift your baby out of the stroller and put her to sleep on a flat surface.

- Try not to share a bed with your baby but make sure that the cot or the bassinet is near you.

Do not keep too many soft items toys, bumper pads, pillows, or blankets inside the cot. These might suffocate your baby if she somehow rolls over them or gets stuck in loose bedding.

- Never put any positioners or make wedges in your baby's crib.

Make sure that the room is not overheated and do not cover your baby's head. Covering the head might be a common practice during very cold winters, but it increases the chance of suffocation.

Is It Dangerous When Mother Sleeps With The Baby?

Over the past few years, studies have shown that new mothers wish to hold their babies while going to sleep. This particular trend has actually started growing after 1993 by almost 24%.

However, this goes against the advice given by The American Academy of Pediatrics who states that sharing a bed with a baby "should be avoided at all times" especially if the baby is a "[full-]term normal-weight infant younger than four months". The reasons why the American Academy of Pediatrics does not recommend the mother sharing a bed with her baby are stated below:

- Infants who have not yet reached the age of 4 months are exposed to the risk of several sleep-related diseases if this trend is put in practice
- Sudden infant death syndrome or accidental strangulation and accidental suffocation might occur if the baby sleeps with her mother

However, it is instinctive for mothers to hold their babies and cuddle them while sleeping. Babies too, want to be held and what to be near their mothers, at all times. Now, this kind of a mutual pull towards each other is very important and should be assessed before ruling out, sharing a bed with your baby.

James McKenna is an anthropologist who has researched extensively about the sleeping patterns of infants, and according to him, "Human babies are contact seekers. What they need the most is their mother's and father's bodies. This is what's good for their physiology. This is what their survival depends on."

Studies have also shown that the trend of sleeping with the baby is quite old and has been around as long as the species of homo sapiens, itself. Several cultures believe in keeping the baby close to her mother at all times. The Western culture of the baby sleeping separately from her mother is rather alien to them. But keeping traditions and cultural practices aside, the fact remains that the baby feels safer in the mother's arm (similar to the time of breastfeeding) and automatically calms down.

Now, the risks stated by the American Academy of Pediatrics are still very much valid, but recent reports have shown that they vary according to the conditions. For example, mothers need to be careful, and the bed that is being shared cannot be an extremely narrow one or one with lots of pillows and cushions.

Following are a few more points which will help one to understand further why the practice of the mother sleeping with her baby is considered to be a dangerous one.

- The baby might get stuck between the bed and other nearby furniture, like the side table or even the wall.
- Too many heavy blankets or large cushions might suffocate the baby.

- The baby might roll off the bed (common in the later months when the baby is developing her motor skills)
- The baby can get hurt by getting trapped by the footboard or the headboard.
- The mother might smother her baby or end up rolling over her in her sleep.

It is advisable that the mother does not sleep with her baby, but if she is able to take all precautions and create a safe space for the baby in her bed and stay alert at all times, then bed sharing might be an option. Babies will want to be near their mothers at all times, but it is important to remember what is putting their safety at risk. Also, staying alert at night (even when your baby is sleeping through the night) will be rather exhausting. But many parents are able to adapt to this and prefer to have their baby sleeping in their bed.

As an alternative to sharing the bed, parents can choose co-sleeping. Co-sleeping is different because it involves the baby sleeping very near to her mother but not on the same bed. Here, both the baby and the mother can see, touch, smell and hear each other. This creates a very comforting environment for the baby, and can almost recreate the safety of actually being cuddled while sleeping.

Healthy Sleep Habits in the First Month

As a parent, you should know that babies are born with a reverse or opposite clock. That means, they stay asleep in the day time and remain active during the night. This is because when they're in their mother's womb, they're lulled to sleep by mother's daily movement, which they find soothing.

But in the night time, when mom goes to sleep, and there's no movement, they stay awake and move around inside the womb. So, in other words, the mom's movement and activities are babies' only stimuli for sleep.

So when your baby first comes into this world, your job should be to make her get adjusted to the world's natural stimuli for sleep and get into the circadian rhythm. The faster your baby gets adjusted, the easier and hassle-free your life will become.

But unfortunately, it won't happen in the first month of birth. In the first month itself, you won't necessarily be having a plan to teach your baby how to sleep well and devise a routine for her. Even though babies will be sleeping for at least 20 hours or so each day in the first month, it'll be highly irregular. Innately, they'll be waking up in the middle of the night, taking naps throughout the day, and start crying without any particular reason. So for the first four weeks, you'd have to listen to the demands of the baby, rather than trying to impose yours.

Thus, for the first month, pediatricians advise parents to prioritize their baby's health and overall development and not stress too much about sleep schedule because they'll naturally spend at least 20 hours sleeping, albeit irregular. Proper feeding (mostly breastfeeding), proper body functioning, reflexes should be emphasized. But there are definitely some sleep habits which you can help your baby practice in the first month itself.

Observe Your Baby's Sleep Pattern

First thing, you should learn about how your baby actually sleeps, when, how often, the duration of each sleep cycle, waking habits, reason for waking -- just about everything. When you observe all of these aspects, you can develop a bedtime routine two months down the road. As your baby isn't acquainted with outdoor stimuli for falling asleep, inspect if your baby is actually responding to any stimuli for sleep. If so, you can incorporate this into the bedtime routine you're about to develop.

Also in the first month, you'd have to make sure that they're meeting their sleep quota of at least 18 to 20 hours without disturbances. This is extremely vital for brain and overall physical development.

Feed On Demand

A happy stomach is necessary for your baby to sleep properly. 1-month olds need food once every two hours because of their small stomach size. That's the primary reason babies can't sleep for 4 or 5 hours straight without being alerted by their stomach.

So remember to feed her properly when he's awake and also when she gets out of her sleep in the night.

Healthy Sleep Habits in Months 3-4

Babies after two months have crossed the newborn phase and are ready to get accustomed to their outer environment. It is really the time to impose certain healthy sleeping habits on your baby, and in most cases, they respond exceedingly well.

When babies enter into their 3rd month, they undergo a phase of rapid development, both physically and mentally. The major development milestone that most babies hit is hand-eye coordination. They're able to open and shut their hand, can play with toys, and can sense their environment and react to it. They also gain muscle strength during this period. Their neck muscle, in particular, is able to support their head without wobbling. The upper body, chest, and arms also become strengthened considerably.

When they hit three months, they set into a schedule, which is relieving for most parents given that they won't have to deal with the irregularities of their baby's sleeping habits at the extreme level.

The first thing to note is that the daily sleeping requirement for a 3-months old drop to 15-16 hours per day as opposed to 18 hours per day for newborns. The 15-hour time frame includes both nighttime sleep and daytime naps.

Sleep Training for 3-Month Old Babies

Babies in their 3rd month are more receptive to sleep adjustments. They're starting to get into their body's circadian rhythm and sleep more at night than during the day.

The main purpose of sleep training is to stretch the night sleep hours and make her sleep through the night peacefully. To accomplish this feat, you'd need to train your baby and bring some changes to her lifestyle.

First, try to reduce her total day nap time, and pump those hours into the night sleep instead. If she oversleeps in the day, then she'll find it harder to get to sleep early and easily. The main focus should be a 3-4 hour window before you put her to sleep. Try to keep her awake during this time period.

Even though babies are not really ready for a dedicated bedtime routine in their 3rd month, you can still start the process with a routine comprising of 2 or 3 activities. Dimming the lights when it's time to sleep and cuddling her for a few minutes are some simple activities. She can easily get accustomed to the soothing sensation and take it up as a cue for sleeping.

Feeding is an important part of uninterrupted sleep. Even though they need food every 2-3 hours, feed her till her tummy is full before she goes to bed.

Between 3-4 months, you should also try to make her get accustomed to self-soothing where babies learn to sleep on their own rather than with the help of a parent. To do this, put her to bed when she is in drowsy state and hasn't completely slept. Let her fall asleep on her own. This will help them when they wake up in the night. They'll be able to fall themselves back to sleep.

Healthy Sleep Habits in the Second Month

In the second month, your baby is still a newborn, but is into the final phase of it and starting to get a sense of the outer world and its own baby's personality. She will be more active, and you'll experience better parent-baby coordination.

From the second month onwards, your baby's sleeping pattern will be predictable than the first month, but still not enough to develop a sleeping routine around. Chances are you might have to leave the sleeping pattern to your baby and observe from a distance.

A lot of developmental changes take place during the second month. Your baby gains more control over their bodies and can hold their head steadier and upright while lying on their tummies. This is an important child development milestone. They also gain a bit more control over their feelings, and the reason for their cry becomes apparent, whether it's hunger or other comfort issues.

But they still require at least 16-18 hours of sleep, if not 20 hours. And as a responsible parent, you should make sure that they achieve that milestone without any disturbances. Proper sleep is still vital for brain development. But just in case of the first month, the sleeping pattern will be sporadic, though to a lesser degree. What remains constant is that they'll be sleeping for 18 hours, would require food every two or three hours, and will be waking up for a period of 2 hours before falling back to sleep.

To develop a proper sleep schedule for your 2-months old baby, you'd have to wait for some more weeks or months. But in the meantime, you can encourage your newborn to sleep better.

While needing at least 18 hours of sleep, you shouldn't disrupt their natural sleeping pattern. So the best thing you can do is to observe their pattern and plan your schedule around it. They'll still be affixed to their reverse sleeping pattern when they used to sleep in the daytime and remain active during the night. So chances are she won't be familiar with the day-night sleeping pattern that we follow even after one month.

By observing their pattern, you can figure out the stimuli that your baby consider as a cue to fall asleep. More often than not, it'd be a full tummy following which babies naturally doze off. The data gathered will help you devise a bedtime schedule sometime afterward.

As they gain more control over their body, you'll find it easier to put them back to sleep by soothing them or making your presence felt. But you can try to not take her out of the crib, instead rub her forehead gently and teach her the art of self-soothe.

Also, remember to feed them properly every 2-3 hours. If they wake up in the middle of the night, then most probably it's because of hunger. In the second month, breastfeeding is still the best food you can offer to your baby.

Healthy Sleep Habits in Months 4-12

When babies hit 4 months, they gain the ability to follow a more conscientious bedtime routine. At this stage, they're referred to as infants and have passed the newborn phase. It's the time to teach your infant how to sleep through the night. So you can feel a bit relieved knowing that you're done with all the sleepless nights, and if things work out well, you can have a full good night's sleep as well.

By month 4, your baby's internal clock or circadian rhythm has started to take shape. She's starting to comprehend that days are meant for playing around and night are meant for sleeping. At this stage, their minimum daily sleep quota has dropped to 14 hours from 16-18 hours the previous month.

The night hours can easily accommodate 8 of those 14 hours, and by the time they hit six months, they can sleep for 9-10 hours uninterrupted. In fact, an uninterrupted 8 hours of sleep becomes necessary for brain development. Rest of the hours can be met during the day time.

Establish a Bedtime Routine

By month 4, a bedtime routine becomes a necessity rather than an option. As baby starts to develop circadian rhythm, they are more than open to getting used to a sleep schedule. You'll notice that he's showing signs of sleepiness more or less at the same time every day. You should capitalize on this and develop a bedtime routine around this time to push your baby to sleep.

Your bedtime routine should ideally include 4-5 activities and should be no more than 30 minutes in duration. Feeding her properly before bedtime is crucial too.

By the 4th month, you should strictly impose a self-soothing rule for your baby to follow. For example, after going through the bedtime routine, just put her in her crib, leave the room, and allow her to fall asleep on her own.

Similarly, if she's awake in the night, don't pick her out of her crib or start feeding her. If you've fed her well before sleep, she is not really hungry. In fact, it's common for them to wake up during the night. Just make your presence felt for a few minutes and encourage your child to go back to sleep. Even if you don't notice, most babies after six months wake up around five times in the middle of the night but go back to sleep on their own. By six months to 1 year, this habit will help them to sleep through the night without your intervention.

By the time they're about to hit one year, they should get accustomed to the habit of sleeping 8-10 hours peacefully through the night. So pretty much everything would be on autopilot, so to speak, and you'd have just to keep this on track.

4-month olds should get a colic disease check. If your baby cries for a prolonged period without any reason, then it might be colic. Even though it fades away after six weeks, it's really scary for parents for the time it persists.

Nap Time: Strategies That Work

Newborns often sleep for a very long time, only waking up when they are hungry. At this age, they have no concept of day and night, and cannot distinguish between the two. However, as the months go by, with more developmental changes, it will become important to have a healthy pattern or proper sleeping and feeding schedules.

During this time, you can slowly start to teach your baby the difference between day and night, so that her sleep schedules are regulated. It is very important to build healthy sleeping habits, as these will lead up to your baby sleeping throughout the night without fussing. However, new mothers often struggle to establish these habits and get their babies to settle down. Given below are a few such strategies that will help to get your baby to sleep and also regulate her nap times.

- Use the lights in the house strategically.

The lights that you have in your home can help in influencing your baby's biological clock when used correctly. When a room is brightly lit, your baby will immediately be more alert and attentive. On the other hand, if you switch off a few lights, and the room becomes dark, then this will trigger the release of melatonin.

Melatonin is a hormone that makes one sleepy. Therefore, if you keep the house or the room your baby is in brightly lit during the day and dark during the night, you baby will soon figure out which is the time stay awake and which is the time to sleep. Once you start doing this, create a schedule for the nap times, and in the evening, start dimming the lights so that your baby gradually becomes sleepy, instead of switching off lights all at once, as the latter might startle her.

When your baby is napping during the day, do not darken the room but allow lots of natural light to come in. Let her sleep in a room that has enough light. This way, your baby will understand that it is a day, and the naptime is of a short period.

Your baby will also start identifying day and night with the amount of sleep she is getting. Ideally, you want your baby to sleep through the night, but not sleep for more than a few hours during the day. Identifying the various intensities of light will help your baby adjust to this sooner.

If you decide to put in night light, then make sure it is not a very harsh one and if your baby wakes up in the middle of the night, then do not immediately switch on all the lights. Instead, switch on this night light, or dimmed lights and slowly soothe your baby back to sleep.

- Put your baby to bed when she is drowsy.

Understanding when your baby is drowsy is not really difficult (except for mothers who are breastfeeding their babies, as babies tend to fall asleep while being nursed). Look for cues as babies when sleepy, tend to rub their eyes, yawn or generally quieten down. If you do notice any of these, then put your baby to bed and let your baby drift off to sleep on her own.

Babies who are able to do this, are also able to soothe themselves while sleeping and usually do not get very fussy. Also, if you wait till your baby is asleep, then putting her down to bed after that might actually be difficult. The slightest movement can wake your baby up or cause some discomfort. So, to avoid that, it is best to put your baby to bed once she starts nodding off.

Do not play with your baby before bedtime or even make eye contact once you have put her to bed.

Babies become alert at the slightest of things, and it is very important for them to calm down before bed. If they are too excited, then they will not be able to sleep, which might disrupt the usual schedule.

One thing that babies find engaging is eye contact. When you make eye contact with your baby, it is automatically a signal and it will hold your baby's attention. She will think its playtime, and therefore become completely alert. When you do this and engage your baby's attention, your baby will easily come out of her drowsy state and it will be very difficult for you to settle her down. Also, this does not allow your baby to get sound sleep.

Before bedtime, try calming your baby. Do not allow her to be too energetic in the evening (as bedtime approaches) and do not talk loudly or play loud music. You can sing a lullaby or gently stroke your baby's forehead so that she becomes calm and slowly starts to nod off.

Wait for some time before going to your baby when she wakes up in the middle of the night.

Sometimes, babies wake up in the middle of the night and fuss a little. However, you do not need to always attend. It is a good opportunity for your baby to calm down on her own and soothe herself back to sleep again. Babies often gurgle in the sleep but they do not completely wake up.

If you keep going to your baby every time she fusses a little, then you will simply encourage your baby to develop the habit of waking up frequently in the middle of the night. However, it is also necessary to keep a check and step in if you see your baby getting too frantic. Wait for a while and see if she does calm down. If your baby becomes more stressed, then immediately cuddle and soothe her back to sleep.

Should Baby Cry It Out Before Sleeping?

No parent wants to see their baby cry, but according to some researchers crying before sleep can actually improve your baby's night sleep. Cry-it-out or CIO is a sleep training approach where you let your child cry for extended periods of time following which she goes to sleep and is able to sleep well through the night.

While this practice is still shrouded in controversy, many parents across the globe are giving it a try, and the results reported thus far are mixed.

What is Cry-It-Out Sleep Training?

Cry-it-out is an umbrella term that refers to varying crying practices for babies before bedtime. What differentiates each practice from the other is the length for which a baby cries and sympathy that the parent show. The most rigid form of this training involves leaving your baby completely alone while he's crying and letting her go to sleep on her own. While in the gentler version, you visit your baby intermittently and soothe them to bed.

A form of this technique was first introduced to the masses by pediatrician Richard Ferber in his book "Solve Your Child's Sleep Problem" which came out in 1985, and expanded in 2006.

Why is Cry-It-Out Important for Babies?

The importance of CIO is closely tied to the bedtime routine. These are a set of activities which lead up to your baby's sleep. The main purpose of these activities cues your child's brain that it's time to sleep.

Toddlers generally, after four months, have a hard time going to sleep on their own. If they're not exposed to a bedtime routine, they may not sleep as fast as you'd like. And even if they sleep, he'll wake up in the middle of the night screaming for your help.

On average, 4-months old babies wake up five times in the night, during their sleep. If she's not accustomed to the bedtime routine and hasn't learned self-soothing, then chances are she'll not be able to put herself back to sleep.

Therefore, developing and practicing the bedtime routine is extremely important.

CIO is a part of the bedtime routine, and if you include it, it'll be the final activity following which your baby will go to sleep.

The whole theory behind Cry-It-Out is if babies get used to the caring custom of parents like soothing, rocking, or nursing to put them to bed, then they'll never learn how to sleep without their intervention. As mentioned earlier, they wake up five times in night on average. So they'll cry for help every time.

Also, scientifically since our body craves for sleep when we cry, it might induce sleep-related hormones in babies as well, thus helping them to fall aslccp.

How to Practice the Cry-It-Out Technique?

If your baby is facing sleeping troubles, then you can employ this technique. The best age range to start CIO training is between 4 to 6 months, but it varies based on your baby's overall development.

4-month old babies are at a better position to absorb the skills necessary for self-soothing and get acquainted with the bedtime routine.

To start wakes with, you don't have to be extremely harsh with leave the child completely alone for her to sleep. Instead, return to her crib intermittently and assure her of everything being okay.

This is called the Ferber Method CIO, also known as "graduated extinction". Here's how this method looks like:

- Complete your normal bedtime routine like playing, feeding, soothing, first.
- Put your baby in her crib, dim the lights, and leave the room.
- If she starts crying, let her do so for 5 or 6 minutes.
- Re-enter her room and make your presence felt. But don't take her out of her crib. Just rub her head, hands for a minute or so, or till she calms down.
- Again leave the room.
- If you hear her cry again, let the duration be 8-10 minutes this time before you re-enter.
- Again, repeat the process for 2-3 times with expanding the intervals.

In the beginning, it's almost impossible for parents to leave their babies like this. Getting used to this method will take a couple of days or weeks.

The harsher technique is called the Weissbluth Method developed by Dr. Marc Weissbluth. In this method, you don't get to enter the baby's room and calm her down. Instead, you let her cry for as long as she wants to.

Another popular CIO technique is the Babywise Approach developed by Dr. Robert Bucknam and described thoroughly in the book "On Becoming Babywise." While this doesn't directly advocate for crying it out before bedtime, it recommends something called a sleep-eat-play cycle. While getting used to this new cycle, babies are innately going to cry. And Dr. Bucknam says it's normal and you should let your baby cry to get used to this cycle. He further asserts that by following this method, your baby won't stand in need of nursing or soothing while going to bed. Her brain will get aligned with its circadian rhythm.

Is the Cry-It-Out Technique Safe?

The motive behind cry-it-out is to teach your child to sleep on her own and with crying being just being a mere transitioning phase. Crying is not the ultimate goal of CIO but making her sleep on her own is.

When your baby learns to sleep without your intervention while practicing CIO, the habit of crying will gradually fade away leaving behind only the end result -- baby going to sleep on her own. So in that regard, CIO is pretty much safe in the long run, and for some parents, necessary or vital.

That being said, CIO is extremely difficult for parents in the beginning at an emotional level. But if you stick with it for a few days, you'll reap the benefits.

Teaching the Difference Between Night And Day to Your Baby

Babies need to be able to differentiate between day and night. They spend nine months inside a dark womb, thus they're completely unaware of the concept of day and night. In the fetus stage, they spend the majority of the nine months in hibernation or sleeping. It's only after the 9th week of pregnancy that they show signs of any movement. Gradually, it speeds up and towards the birth time, the movement becomes obvious.

As far as sleep pattern is concerned, they're born with a reversed sleep cycle. Some babies inside the womb remain active for the majority of the night when their mom goes to sleep and sleeps during the day when the mother is active. So babies develop a sleep-wake cycle even before they're born. And when they're finally born, they continue on with the cycle for the first few weeks or months of their birth.

By the time they're into their third trimester, they experience REM sleep just like adults where they have dreams in their sleep. After a month, they develop non-REM sleep or quiet sleep. They sleep for a few hours and become active for a few hours before going back to sleep again. But this is highly irregular and cannot be generalized.

When babies are born, they sleep almost 20 hours a day in the first month. Their sleeping pattern is highly irregular and wakes up in the night to be fed. This is exhausting for almost all parents.

But from the third or fourth month, they begin to sleep through the night with ease. But this transition isn't completely natural. Parent's intervention plays an important part. This intervention is in the form of sleep training designed for toddlers.

One of the main components of this training is helping your newborn to get acquainted with the nuances of the outer world, especially the day-night pattern and what it means.

How to Teach Your Baby Difference between Day and Night?

Babies naturally get acquainted with the day-night pattern, and after a few months, they'll be sleeping more during the night than day. By three to four months, they should be able to sleep 7-8 hours through the night without causing disturbances.

But to speed up this process, you can (and should) employ certain training techniques to make the transition faster.

Here are some tips for teaching your baby:

- Expose your baby to the natural sunlight

Sun is the natural lighting source, and since the origin of life, it has been determining day and night on earth. So the first step would be to expose your child to the sun rays and lights, preferably for the full day. The rays will also energize them and make them play cheerfully.

Keep the shades and curtains open and let the sunlight brighten your baby's room. Blocking the sunlight won't help your child's day-night distinguishing ability. Take her outside your house for a short period of time either in the morning or in the evening.

- Let there be darkness at night

If you're exposing your child to sunlight during the daytime, then expose her to utter darkness at night time. This way after a long active day of playing, your baby will associate darkness with sleep. Don't use bulbs either that are known to emit blue light wavelengths which can disrupt sleep by accelerating the presence of a chemical called melatonin in the body.

If your baby wakes up in the middle of the night and you need to feed her, use the dimmest light possible that doesn't emit any blue light wavelength, or don't turn on the TV either. Lull her back to sleep with minimal light simulation.

- Silence is essential too

Not only you have to prohibit lighting at night hours, but noise should be at a minimal level as well. Babies can easily get disturbed by loud noises around them and this can disrupt their sleep – spoiling the entire setting.

Once there's complete silence in the night, she'll start associating silence with sleep. When there's complete silence, your baby can go to sleep quicker. Silence combined with darkness is the perfect recipe for training your child to get used tonight and then associate it with sleep.

- Try to minimize daytime naps

If you want your child to sleep peacefully through the night, then cutting down on daytime naps is crucial. If she oversleeps during the day, then she'll find it harder to associate night with sleep and go back to her previous day-night cycle that she was undergoing inside the womb. Oversleeping will also refrain her from sleeping early.

To avoid oversleeping, make her play with toys or with you for an extended period of time, especially during the hours before bedtime. It is recommended to have at least 3 hours gap between her last nap and bedtime. That's why a bedtime routine is in place.

But that's not to say you deprive her completely of daytime naps. They'll still need 14-15 hours of sleep per day, and it's almost impossible to meet that quota in a single stretch.

- Use biological LED bulbs

Humans have always been a light-sensitive creature. We easily get disturbed or distracted by even dim lighting. All artificial lighting like bulbs, TV screen, mobile phone screen emit blue wavelength light that encourages melatonin production in the body. This chemical is known to disrupt sleep.

Biological LED bulbs don't emit these blue wavelength lights which can produce melatonin in the body. So next time when you consider night lighting arrangement, it's wise to purchase biological LED bulbs or those that filter blue light wavelength. Your baby will be able to better cope up with the natural day-night sleeping pattern.

Managing Baby Sleep When You Have Twins/Triplets

Managing sleep for a single infant is not easy, and the task becomes even hassle fully if you have twins or triplets. Keeping up with the sleeping pattern of each of the baby is a daunting task.

Well, nothing to worry as the following content will help you get more information regarding the process of managing the baby's sleep when you have twins or triplets.

- Be practical and realistic about sleep

Obviously, every parent would want their twins or triplets to sleep at the same time or at least have a similar sleeping pattern. In fact, many parents make it their goal to eventually get babies on the same sleeping schedule.

But let's be honest and practical here! You need to understand and accept the fact that it may not happen right away and will take some time. As parents, you just need to hold on to the fact, that it will happen and may take a couple of months. That means your babies will eventually get used to the sleeping schedule, you just need to be calm and patient as well as give them some time to adjust naturally.

- It is recommended to have one crib in the beginning

As parents, you definitely want to give the best of everything to your babies like the separate crib, toys, two car seats, a double stroller, etc. But, there is a catch here. If you have twins or triplets, experts say it is better to have one crib in the beginning- for initial days. This process encourages them to develop a similar sleeping pattern. So, try to put the babies in a single crib and see if they are able to sleep together. The interesting reason behind this as quoted by experts is that babies sleep better when they know the other is close by. It gives them a feeling of safety.

There are a few points which one needs to remember here-

- o Put the babies head to toe at opposite ends of the cot, while they are sleeping. This reduces the possibility of an accident and is a safer way.
- o The sleep of newborn babies does not depend on their age, but their weight. Thus, don't panic; they will start sleeping through the night when they are ready. You have to maintain a safe, quiet, and calm environment to encourage them to sleep through the night.
- o The most important point to note here is that you should separate the crib of your twins or triplets once, they start to move a lot or stroll. Because at that point, keeping them in a single crib is probably a bad idea.
- The key step for getting twins or triplets to sleep at the same time is- double-duty feeding

New mothers of twins or triplets should at first try to get their cuties on a fine feeding schedule. You can take the advice on the same from your pediatrician or another family doctor. When a baby has a fixed schedule of eating and /her stomach is full, she will sleep. And one should let them snooze if they are feeding every four hours. Now, the crucial point to note here for parents who have twins or triplets is that- they must try to have a fix feeding schedule for all their babies. This way the chances of them to fall asleep or feel drowsy at the same time increases to various levels.

Once you have fed the babies and then, burped them as well, just allow them to play. They will eventually get tired and will feel sleepy. It may take a bit of time for the babies to feel drowsy at the same time, but fixing the feeding schedule for twins, triplets helps in a great way.

Once you feel the babies are feeling drowsy after they have fed and played, swaddle them and then lay them to sleep. Each parent can swaddle a baby or you can also take help of the nanny. Swaddling helps the babies to have a better sleep. As far as having a fixed schedule for feeding and other queries related to it, you must talk to your doctor and they can guide you well enough.

- Try to nap your twins at the same time

We all know and understand that being parents to twins or triplets is a lot of tasks but once you get a grip of it, it just becomes easier and easier. According to the experts of the American Academy of Pediatrics, twins sleep on entirely different spaces.

But parents can try a trick here. You can try to put them down for nap simultaneously. Now, there are chances that one of the babies can take some extra time as well as soothing (the process of rubbing backs or singing soft lullabies) to fall asleep finally. Well, it's okay. But you have to try and manage to put them simultaneously for a nap.

The result of this process is that in a few months, your twins or triplets will develop a scheduled or organized sleeping pattern. Sounds great, isn't it?

- If one of the twin or triplets is up for feeding or playing, wake the others too

It can be hard as parents to wake up a peacefully sleeping baby, but if you have twins and triplets and you want them to have a similar sleeping pattern, then you got to do whatever it takes. And, if you don't do so, then you will end up just exhausting yourself in managing different sleeping schedules of your baby.

So, you will have to wake the other baby/babies if one is up for feeding. You will observe that within a few days or weeks, the babies start to get hungry at the same time and probably doze off at a similar time. Well, that's the jackpot you must aim for. It not only gives more time for yourself but you also get more time to bond with your newborn, which is the most important thing for the .new mothers.

Now, there is a possibility that you prefer nursing your babies on-demand, through the night. In such a case, it is important to remember that it may just take your twins or triplets longer than their singleton counterpart to doze through the pee hours.

- Develop a strong bedtime routine to help twins sleep

A nighttime routine is important for all the babies, and especially for triplets or twins. Now, if one of the babies is up, then her protests, cries, or movements may wake other twin or other two babies in case of triplets and so on. The end result of all this is- you have not one but 2 or 3 cranky babies, and this can make your life messy and extremely tiresome.

So, in order to avoid this scary situation, you have to start a routine for your twins and triplets. For this maintaining an apt sleeping environment is amicable. For this, you can dim the room lights, sing or play lullabies, read books and then swaddle them as well. This offers the babies a cozy and safe environment to doze to dreamland.

Remember to repeat this routine every night on the same time, this way the babies gets tuned to the routine and as soon as the lullabies start to play, and the lights are dim they know that it is bedtime. And, finally, they get scheduled to a proper sleeping routine.

- Start with making small goals

New parents can be restless at times and want their babies to sleep uninterrupted throughout the night. The great tip for being good new parents is- be patient.

This a well-known fact that twins or triplets have comparatively less weight as compared to single babies. Thus, they take more time to get adjusted to the sleeping pattern. There is another issue with twins and triplets that they have a tendency to wake each other throughout the night if they are in the same crib.

Under such circumstances, you need to be patient and make smaller goals in order to develop a similar sleeping pattern for your twins or triplets. You may start by adjusting the feeding schedule. For example- shifting from four feedings in a night to three. You can also teach your babies to soothe themselves back to sleep with the help of pacifier.

Finally, you must divide and conquer. There may be chances that only one of the twin or triplet learns to sleep through the night first. Under this case, you should let that baby sleep in a different room, away from other sibling/siblings. This way, the sleeping baby won't wake up, and you can work with the other sibling's sleeping pattern. Slowly your twins and triplets will learn to sleep at the same time.

Thus, this is a shout out to all the new parents who have twins or triplets, follow the above mentioned key points in order to manage the sleep of your twins and triplets. These points can help you in all possible ways.

Sleep Training Techniques for Your Baby

1. Check-Console-Check

Your baby has your fragrance and aura set in the body system, and her senses tell her when you are around. Sleep training techniques involve your little one to get over the comfort of your presence and fall asleep without relying on your shoulder, arms or presence. The check-console-check method is based on the routine that you slowly increase the time of checking up on your baby and decrease the time you console her.

Put your baby into the crib with her nightclothes on. Lay her down with her security blanket or favorite teddy bear and leave the room. Stay outside for 30 seconds or a minute and then check up on her. If she cries in that time, console her a bit but not more than 10 seconds and leave the room again. This time, stay out for twice the time as before and then go again to check up on her. Do not talk to her if she does not crib or cry.

Know the difference between checking and consoling. For the entire time that you are out, do not go back if you hear your baby crying before the duration ends. Also, the consoling time cannot exceed 50% of the time that you were away. If you were out for 2 minutes, stay for 30 seconds to calm her down. Remember that consoling should not involve picking her up in your arms. Talk to her in sweet voices, make faces, pat her, or sing a song. If you take her out of the crib, the whole training would be vile, and you would be back to square one.

Let the baby know that you are not going to give in to the demands and crying, and she will ultimately exhaust herself and fall asleep after sometime. Surprisingly, this routine trains a baby to fall asleep on her own in just a few days.

This method is also known by other names like progressive waiting, Ferber method, graduated extinction or the interval method.

2. Cry It Out

The Cry It Out or the CIO method is widely famous and is known to be the most effective one too. But it requires a mother to be strong enough to see her baby cry for long.

Understand that this training technique does not aim at making your child cry. The goal of this method is to let your child adjust to sleeping on her own. You give her enough time to soothe herself to sleep at bedtime. Your only role is to monitor her through timely checks that are spread over minutes.

On day one, wait until your baby is physically and emotionally tired and ready to fall asleep. It should be around the time that you plan on putting her to sleep every night. Lay her down in the crib while she is awake yet sleepy. Turn off the lights, wish her goodnight, say some sweet words, and leave the room. You are going to hear crying voices once you leave. Stay strong and convince your mind and heart not to return. Stay out for 3 minutes on the clock, and then return. Soothe her with your voice but do not pick her up. Leave the room in a minute even if she is crying. Repeat this for 5 and 10 minutes intervals. She will eventually exhaust herself and understand that you are not going to pick her up and comfort her in your arms. This is different from the check-console-check routine since you would be leaving for longer durations and not be patting her this time.

Note that the age of the baby can vary from 4 to 6 months, and sometimes even more before you should give this method a try. Since the needs and health of each child are different, it cannot be concluded what age is best to adapt to the CIO technique.

3.   Take the Chair

All your child needs is your presence. You would have noticed how happy she is when you are in the room and the screams that come the moment you step out. Even if she is minding her own business, she just needs to feel your presence around her.

The Chair method uses this fact to develop independent sleeping skills in a baby. It does not involve you leaving the room, so there would be much less crying. Your little one would stay right in front of you, just not in your arms.

When your baby is drowsy yet awake, put her down in her bed. Take a chair and sit beside her. Read a book or listen to some music. Your baby would look up to you and even cry for taking her in your arms. Soothe her with your words and sweet voices. Then continue with your work. Stay there till she falls asleep on her own. On the next night, place the chair a little further from the previous night. Sit there and watch her fall asleep with her own efforts. Keep increasing the distance every night between your chair and her bed or crib. By the time your chair gets out of the door, your baby will have adapted to sleeping on her own.

She may take some time, which means you would need to have patience and the heart to see her cry. You can shush her from the chair itself and watch her fall asleep. And the end result of seeing her sleep on her own will take the guilt away and give you peace and happiness. You would finally be able to get some rest and sound sleep.

4. Up, Down, Shush, Pat

Not all mothers are strong while most babies are stubborn. They would cry to the extent of heavy tears and loud noises until you HAVE to pick them up. There is no assigned age as to when a baby stops being dependent and starts doing things on her own.

The 'up, down, shush, pat' sleep training method is comforting for the baby and the mother as well. It works best for the crying lovers who have accepted that tears and screams can get them what they want.

This technique also involves leaving a sleepy toddler in the crib and leaving the room. Once you hear her cry, you go to the room, pick her up, shush her, pat her, and finally put her back in the crib. Leave the room after that. The next time she cries, take some time to go back and repeat the same process.

What you need to remember is that your baby should not fall asleep in your arms. Put her back in the crib the minute you feel she is dozing off. This way she would remember that she will get to sleep only when she is in her bed and not in her arms. Increase the time of returning to her in the following days, and spend little time in the 'up, down, shush, pat' routine. You will start seeing the results in a few days. The crying will be controlled and your baby will get accustomed to sleeping on her own.

5.   Fade the Bedtime-Hour

There is usually a pattern of sleeping time that is followed by a person. Your baby will also have a sleeping window when she would doze off almost every day. If you keep a diary and note down the time each night when she falls asleep, you would notice that it lies within a window of 15-20 minutes. If you try to put her to bed before that time, she would just cry and ask for your comfort before she finally sleeps at her own time.

Therefore you can use the very efficient sleep training method of delaying the time when you put the baby to sleep. Do not give her the window to make a fuss or call for comfort. Put her into bed exactly at the time that you know she dozes off every day. In other words, delay the time when you try to make her sleep. There would be less crying and less fuss for you. This trick would work effortlessly since she would be too tired to stay up and cry.

Keep doing this for a couple of nights. When she starts adapting to the routine, which would be probably after a week, shift her bedtime to 15 minutes earlier. She would herself adjust to the new time within a few days. You can keep fading the bedtime hour by 15 minutes till your baby reaches a suitable sleeping hour. Since there would be hardly any crying, you would be able to resist taking her into your arms without many efforts.

6. Hybrid Approach

Every human is different, and so is a baby. While the sleep training techniques work most of the times, some babies still cannot learn to sleep on their own even after applying them. In such cases, you can use a hybrid approach and try two methods together.

For instance, if you go for the fading chair and bedtime-hour routine together, you would be sitting beside your baby after you put her down to sleep at the time she dozes off. Over the next few nights, you keep shifting the chair towards the door and the sleeping time to an earlier time. This gives you the benefit of two training techniques in one go.

You should be smart enough to realize which technique or combination would work the best for your baby. A mother is the only one who knows her child and all habits. There is no better person around to decide which sleep training technique would be best suited to your baby.

7. Silent Return

If your baby has started to crawl or walk and still does not sleep without you, you should consider the silent return technique to make her sleep. It is a simple approach which involves putting her to bed each time she walks out of it.

Once you have tucked her in, she would have a tendency to come running to you. Pick her up and tuck her back in without saying a word. Do not comfort her, do not sing to her, do not say anything- just silently return her to bed. After a few rounds, she will eventually get tired and go to sleep. Over a few days or weeks, she would understand that this is the way it is going to be and would start sleeping on her own.

How to Settle Your Baby

Parents learn about swaddling their infants from nurses available in a hospital. It usually involves a blanket, which is wrapped snugly around your infant's body, thus resembling her mother's womb. This provides a soothing sensation to the baby. As per the AAP, it states that swaddling is an effective method for promoting sleep in infants and calming them down.

However, if you have plans for swaddling your child at home, follow these important guidelines to ensure that what you're doing is safe.

SIDS or Sudden Infant Death Syndrome is a real problem. Protect your baby from this by ensuring you always place it on its back when you put it down to sleep. Following this guideline is important, especially when the baby is lying in a swaddled position. Certain studies claim an increased accidental suffocation risk and higher SIDS occurrences when infants are swaddled while being placed upon their stomach during sleep, or even if they accidentally roll onto the abdomen region.

When Should One Stop Swaddling Their Infants

It is recommended that parents stop swaddling their kids before they turn 2 months old. This is around the time when the baby starts to intentionally roll. Babies should be placed on their backs and monitored carefully, ensuring their risks of accidentally rolling over are minimal.

Be Aware of the Risks

New parents ought to be aware that swaddling does carry certain amounts of risks to it. Swaddling may curb the arousal abilities of a baby, making it harder for your baby to awake easily. Parents are fans of swaddling for this feature - The baby is led to sleep longer without waking up soon. However, decreased arousal comes with its own set of challenges and is theorized to be a major factor behinds deaths related to SIDS.

Sleep Recommendations for Maximizing Sleep from AAP

AAP suggests that parents follow its safe sleep suggestions every possible time when they lay down their baby for sleeping during nighttime or even during naps.

- Ensure the baby is placed with its back facing downwards during sleep. Monitor it well, making sure that it does not roll over itself while being swaddled.

- Don't place any blankets in the crib of your baby. Swaddling blankets or even loose blankets, which become unwrapped, can completely cover the face of your baby, increasing suffocation risks.

- When you buy products that state they can reduce SIDS risks, be cautious regarding these claims. Specialized sleep products, special mattresses, positioners, and wedges have been studied intensively in recent years. The claims relating to its SIDS risk reduction has been shown to be inconclusive, as per AAP data.

- Babies are safest when placed in their bassinets or cribs. Never place them on your bed, since you may roll over them, causing problems.

- Swaddling has a drawback - namely, and your baby may have increased chances of overheating. Therefore, avoid your baby from heating up too much. Rapid breathing, heat rashes, flushed cheeks, damp hair, and sweating are all symptoms of your baby becoming too hot.

- Be sure to place your baby's crib in a smoke-free location.

- For bedtime and naps, use a pacifier for the baby to suck on that will calm it down.

Ensure Your Baby's Hips Are Loose Enough

Swaddling your baby's hips too tight may cause them to develop news problems in their hip region. Latest studies have stated that tightly wrapping and straightening the legs of a baby can cause hip dysplasia or hip dislocation. This is an abnormal hip joint formation, where thigh bone tops aren't held properly and firmly in place in the hip's socket.

The POSNA, along with AAP's Orthopaedics Section is a vocal promoter of hip-healthy techniques of swaddling, which enable the legs of the baby to bend out properly.

How Do I Swaddle My Baby Correctly?

- First, spread out the blanket flat, with a corner being folded down to initiate swaddling.

- Next, place the baby facing upwards on this blanket. Ensure the head is above the corner that's been folded.

- Straighten its left arm. Wrap the blanket's left corner over its body & tuck between its body's right side and its right arm as well.

- Next, tuck the baby's right arm, folding the blanket's right corner over its body. Place it under its left side.

- Twist or fold the blanket's bottom in a loose manner. Tuck it below the baby's side (Any side will do)

- Ensure that the baby's hips aren't restricted by the swaddling blanket and that they can move. At least 2-3 fingers space between swaddle and the chest of the baby must be provided, as per leading experts.

Child Care Centers Swaddling

A few childcare centers might have policies against swaddling babies who are placed into their care. These policies are due to increased SIDS risks or suffocation risks possible if your baby starts rolling over while being swaddled. Hip dysplasia and overheating risks are also possible.

It is recommended that parents wait at least three months before enrolling their infants into a daycare center. Swaddling ought to be phased out before this period ends since babies begin increasing their active period and start rolling.

Studies have shown that when babies with no prior history of being swaddled undergo this, they are all shown to have different reactions when swaddling is done to them for the first time. While babies can be brought into swaddling correctly as it can even help soothe and comfort the baby into a sound sleep, when placed in new environments during an older stage with different caregivers, babies begin turning more active and start rolling. This turns the whole practice into a more risky and challenging venture.

In conclusion

While the benefits of swaddling your baby to help it settle down cannot be underestimated, there are also several guidelines that one has to follow before the baby benefits from it completely. Parents must take care that their route for ensuring an easier life doesn't wind up affecting the baby. Using swaddling after following appropriate guidelines ensures longer, peaceful times for you and the baby, which we suppose, is worth it after all if you're a new parent!

10 Benefits of an Early Bedtime for Your Child

Your child's sleep may be jeopardized, and you might not be having any clue about it. Well, nothing to worry as it can be reduced and corrected by a new habit- an early bedtime.

Often come across parents whose children have no fixed sleeping patter, they have struggle. We rising early in the morning, or they even refrain from going to sleep as well. One of the major and common problems that we need to look at is- children setting and sticking to an early bedtime.

A very important fact to consider here is the benefits offered by an early bedtime. It has the following perks-

- Provides restful sleep to your child,
- And it is much easier to implement than the parents think.

Well, the detailed benefits and advantages of an early bedtime for your child have been mentioned below-

- A relatively healthier child-

According to a study, the babies who have late bedtime routine are at higher risk for language, motor, and social deficits. Further, for children who are going to school, late bedtime can affect their focus, attentiveness, and performance in the class. As per an article published by Pediatricians, there is a correlation between improved sleep and emotional stability in 7- to 11- year-olds.

Other disadvantages of late bedtime include- higher body mass index, poor dietary habits, etc. Thus, a conclusion can be drawn from this, that an early, age-appropriate bedtime can affect your child's health physically, emotionally, and mentally to various levels.

- Less night waking

The later you put your child to bed, the more you increase the chances of night waking. Night waking can be daunting for new parents, and it exhausts them in every possible way. When a child goes through their natural sleep cycle-wake up, they do have the skill to put himself back to sleep. And, as the night goes, it becomes more and more difficult.

- Reduced early rising

There is this myth that parents have – if a child is tired, they will sleep longer. But that is not the case. When the human body is over-tired, it secretes altering hormones, which makes it difficult for them to sleep. Thus, when a child sleeps too late and is over-drowsy, there are chances that they will rise early. The ability to "sleep in" does not typically occur until your child reaches an age of 6.

- Less resistance at bedtime

There are many reasons as to why children resist getting in bed. But, as per the study conducted by the University of California, one of the main reasons for increased resistance during bedtime is poor sleep. All this often leads to temper issues, less energy, poor behavior, low attentiveness, etc. Well, these problems are certainly not unusual for a toddler or preschooler, but they become more intense as they grow up. And, all this happens due to the reason that your child isn't getting to bed early.

- A predictable bedtime

This is a known fact that it is comparatively difficult to set a fixed sleeping pattern for a newborn, and it can take a few months to achieve it. However, this can be done using an easier way. You must try to put your child to bed, early. Well, we know it is not an easy task to do, and your child will push back against it, but with time, the situation will become better and better. And, an early, as well as a fixed bedtime routine, is all you want for your newborns and preschoolers.

- Encourage quality time before bed

As stated by experts, early bedtime forms a good pairing with calm, peaceful, and soothing quality time just before bed. Plus, you get to make sweet memorable moments with your child. You can do this by performing activities like- reading books, poems, singing lullabies or songs and snuggling also helps. Your child will definitely benefit from all these small activities.

- Quicker to sleep

A consistent or fixed routine and early bedtime balance your child's emotional quotient. This allows them to have more sound sleeping time. The preparatory time also signals to your child's body and mind, that it's time to doze off. The body secretes melatonin which is the body's one natural sleep-inducing chemical. This helps your child to quickly and calmly fall asleep.

- Increased overall sleep

Babies and children who get into the habit of going to bed early don't wake up at night and don't rise too early in the morning as well. Thus, they get more and sufficient time to sleep, which is very important for living a healthy life.

- Children get into healthy sleep habits for future

As children grow, they often get into the tendency of sleeping late, but if their body is tuned according to an early bedtime routine, then it rescues them from many issues altogether. Children who get into the habit of sleeping late as they grow, have poorer health and bad digestive system as well.

- A more peaceful and restful evening for you

One of the most important benefits of an early bedtime for parents is that they get to have personal time and enjoy it too. It is a win-win situation for them.

Implementing Early Bedtime Routine

Following are three important steps which you can take to implement an early bedtime for your child-

- Make sure that your baby's bedtime is early as compared to yours. Also, try to take hints from various actions your child does like running eyes, staring, yawning, etc. and immediately try to put them to bed. You get to learn all the signs within a few weeks. It is like being a student of your baby. Tip- Children under the age of 9 must sleep between 7:30 p.m. and 8 p.m.

- Set up a well-planned bedtime routine. In fact, setting up a pattern for putting your child for a nap helps them to sleep on time.

- And, above all an advice which I ask every family to follow- is to strive for consistency when they opt for early bedtime routine for their children and even themselves. Following it thoroughly can help your children to relax and have an amicable emotional, as well as physical health.

Baby crying

Does your baby suddenly start crying while sleeping? In most of the cases, there is nothing serious to be worried about. Crying in sleep is just a phase majority of the babies go through. Sleeping issues among babies are common and are also the biggest challenges of the caregivers. About 30% of toddlers experience sleep-related issues.

What should you do on your part when your baby is crying? Don't feel helpless! Let's first find out the reasons that can make babies cry in their sleep.

- If your baby is making noises in their sleep, including crying. Don't be worried. The baby's body is not used to the regular sleep cycle, which makes them make noises or cry in sleep sometimes.

- As crying is the only form of communication babies know, they cry very often even when they are awake. They tend to cry in sleep too.

- Crying in sleep is not a big concern until your baby is facing some health-related symptoms like pain or any form of sickness.

- As toddlers begin to express themselves better, they also start experiencing dreams and nightmares in their sleep. If your baby tends to move a lot while sleeping or make some sounds, she is probably having night terrors. This could be another reason when your baby cries during sleep.

- Night terrors and nightmares are different. A child experience nightmares during light sleep, whereas night terrors are usually experienced during the early hours of the night when they sleep deeply.

- The probability that your baby is having night terrors are close to none. They usually happen when the baby is sick, agitated, and not getting enough sleep.

What to Do When Your Baby is Crying?

Usually, when a baby cries in sleep, they whine a little and then get back to sleep. Picking them up to soothe them may wake them up, and you may end up in disturbing their sleep. If the baby keeps crying, try talking to them softly and rub their backs to soothe them. This will help them distract from their zoning out and get them back to sleep.

Another way to stop your baby from crying during sleep is by breastfeeding them. Those mothers who make their babies sleep while breastfeeding can do so again when they start crying. However, make sure this does not wake them up. Do so only when they are crying loud enough to risk them waking up.

Analyzing their sleeping pattern can also help you out. Some babies have a habit of letting out a soft cry in deep sleep while some have a habit of crying as they wake up from sleep. A mother or a caretaker who knows his/her child's sleeping pattern can easily know the reason for crying.

If your baby is crying out during sleep while she is teething, it's probably due to her gums paining. In some cases, it is better to talk to the designated doctor to ease the pain.

If your baby wakes up from a nightmare or is crying because of one, soothe them by rubbing their back and by providing them with the assurance that they are not real by being with them.

Situations Which Needs a Doctor's Attention

At what stage you should think over taking your baby to a doctor? Here are some of the situations when you need to do so

- When she is crying out of severe pain

- When there is a sudden change in a child's sleeping habits

- When crying in sleep has become more frequent to the point that it starts to disturb the regular functioning of the baby or the caregiver

- When a caregiver is facing problems in feeding a baby like feeling hungry even after breastfeeding, a bad latch, etc.

The Sleeping Pattern According To Different Ages

The sleeping pattern of your offspring changes as she begins to grow up. It keeps changing after every three years of their life. Babies tend to sleep more than an adult but have shorter sleep cycle and sleep light. Here is how it changes over the years

- Newborn (0 to 1 month)

Confused between day and night, newborn babies keep waking up and sleeping every two to three hours. To set a proper sleeping routine, introduce them to the daylight to regulate it. However, it is still unlikely of them to sleep for the whole night.

- Older newborn (1 to 3 months)

They are still trying to understand the surroundings and will still make your nights sleepless. Their sleep last about 3.5 hours or less. It is peculiar in the older newborn to wake up crying because of hunger.

- Infants (3 to 7 months)

This may differ from baby to baby, but there is a little probability of their sleeping throughout the night. They begin their first step towards setting their sleep routine by taking two naps in a day and later at night.

- Infants (7 to 12 months)

At this time, if you are lucky enough no more sleepless nights for you as your baby will start to sleep throughout the night with one nap in the day. However, it can still vary among different babies.

- Toddlers (12 months and older)

Toddlers need about 12 to 14 hours of sleep a day, including the nap time in the afternoon. Their sleeping pattern will change a lot due to illness or change in routine and experience more crying than usual while sleeping.

The only sole purpose of babies in their early life is sleeping. They may or may not face issues while sleeping as every child has a unique set of traits. There is nothing too serious when your baby is crying while sleeping. Every child goes through this phase, and it's actually a good sign to be normal.

Routines

Routines or schedules are extremely important when it comes to helping your baby develop good habits that will keep her healthy and happy. You can start with bed, bath and feeding routines from a very early age (when your baby is still a new-born).

This will make sure that your baby is able to relate to a pattern from early on and therefore, continue to maintain that routine (with any necessary changes) even as they grow up.

Discussed below are two different sets of routines that you should maintain from early on. These are feeding and napping routine, and bath and bed routine. Now, when you are introducing a bedtime or a naptime routine, it is important to understand when your baby is feeling sleepy.

Therefore, you need to look for sleep cues, and these cues are also discussed later on.

Feeding and Napping Routine

The usual day and night cycle cannot be applied to newborns because they do not have any concept of day and night. A new-born sleeps for most of the time, only waking up when hungry. Now, if you observe a newborn's sleeping pattern, you will find that she is sleeping for about forty-five minutes, before waking up.

But sometimes, they can sleep for longer stretches, like for about three to four hours, before waking up to feed. To create a routine for napping and feeding, try to figure out when your baby is getting. Your baby will usually rub her eyes, yawn, or even fuss a little when she is very tired. Once you take note of the time when your baby is getting drowsy, you can then begin to establish a routine.

- Routine for your new-born

The best routine for new-born is to feed them every two hours or so and then allow them to nap for the rest of the time. You can feed your new-born more frequently during the day, allowing him or her to nap for about an hour before nursing again.

But slow that down in the afternoon and allow a longer nap (for about two to three hours). However, never allow your new-born to sleep for very long in the evening (only a short nap of about thirty to forty minutes). This is because, if your new-born sleeps a lot in the evening, then at night, she will be more alert. Now, at night wake your new-born up twice (allowing three to four hours of sleep in between) and feed him or her.

Now, for bottle-fed babies, feedings should be fewer. This is because the baby formula that you are feeding will need some time to be properly digested. During the day, allow your baby to nap for about an hour before waking up and playing a bit. Do not feed your baby too often, but let a couple of hours go by after each feeding.

This routine is recommended only if your baby is a few weeks old, and at that age, your baby should not be sleeping for more than thirty minutes to an hour, at a stretch. The bedtime feeding schedule should not change, however.

Feed your baby right before bedtime, so that she feels comfortable and full, but wake her up twice during the night (allowing three to four hours of sleep in between) and then settle her down to sleep immediately.

- Routine for babies who are two to four months old

At two months old, your baby will start to sleep more often, for longer stretches at night, while staying awake during the day. Usually, they will sleep for a total of four to six hours during the day and nine to twelve hours during the night.

At this age, you will not be able to set a proper bedtime schedule, as the sleeping patterns will appear quite erratic. When your baby is about two months old, your baby will start developing and growing more, and therefore, she will start eating more. If you are breastfeeding your baby, then remember to nurse him or her, every two to three hours.

But if you are feeding baby formula, then allow more time to pass in between two feedings. Night feedings will still be needed at this stage. Feed your baby once before bedtime, and then include three more feedings during the night, as your baby now has the capacity to consume more. However, if you are feeding your baby some formula, then you can feed him or her twice during the night, as the formula can be quite heavy.

Now once your baby is three to four months old, you will notice that her sleeping pattern has become somewhat regulated. Your baby will now be sleeping for about eleven to twelve hours at night, and you will have to feed him or her only a couple of times during the night. During the day, your baby will be napping for about thirty minutes at a stretch, and even then, the naps will not be very frequent.

At this age, your baby's feedings will also become more consolidated, and night feedings will become quite infrequent. Whether you are breastfeeding your baby or feeding her baby formula, remember to set a few fixed points during the day. Fixed points are fixed timings for naps and feedings.

Having a few fixed points will help you to stick to the routine. For example, keep the morning feeding time fixed at about seven or eight in the morning, and then naptime an hour later. Keep the evening naptime fixed as well, followed by the bedtime. Do not change these times, as any disruption can affect your baby's whole routine.

- Routine for when your baby is five to seven months old

At five months, your baby should be taking about four naps during the day and sleeping for a total of eleven hours during the night. After a couple of months, you will notice that your baby is staying awake for almost the whole day, needing only a couple of short naps. This is also the time when you can introduce solid food to your baby. But if you are breastfeeding your baby, then you will still need to feed your baby several times during the day.

If you start your baby on solid foods, then stick to only about a couple of servings. The solid foods that you can give at this age are baby cereal (1 serving is equivalent to two tablespoons when dry), fruits (1 serving is equivalent to one to two tablespoons) and vegetables (1 serving is equivalent to one to two tablespoons).

At six to seven months old, you need to breastfeed your baby at least five to six times per day. Of you are feeding him or her baby formula, then 24-32 ounces formula should be given. Water is not really necessary as both breast milk and formula will have enough water in them. But, babies often have constipation issues at this (when fed solids), and therefore along with vegetables and baby cereals (a couple of servings of each), you can give fruits like pears and prunes.

- After seven months (eight months to twelve months)

During this time, your baby will already have a working feeding and napping routine. You baby should also be sleeping through the night, which means no night-time feeding. If you are feeding your baby solid food, then increase the servings to three to four during the day. As the months go by, your baby will need very few naps, and you can start giving small amounts of baby cereals, fruits, vegetables and even some portions of protein and dairy.

It is best to primarily breastfeed and include some baby formula during the day (once when your baby wakes up, then once in the late afternoon, and again in the evening before bedtime). Punctuate these feedings, with small snacks of solid foods.

At this age, you will be able to establish a proper bedtime and a proper time to wake up as well. Make sure that neither of these two fixed times is late as that will create an unhealthy sleeping habit.

Bath and Bed Routine

A bath before bedtime can be very soothing and relaxing for your baby, especially during the summer months. Bathing will calm your baby and help them settle down for sleep. Also, giving a bath will strengthen your bond with your baby, which is extremely comforting and can prepare your baby for a good night's sleep.

Forgiving a bath, set a particular time (preferably around 6/6:30). This should be after your baby has had the bedtime feed. Now, fill a tub with lukewarm water and add some gentle, sweet-smelling baby bath product. Babies love water, and you can let them splash about for a while before you begin washing.

Always use a soft washcloth to gently rub some soap and clean your baby. While you do this, you can sing or even talk to your baby to keep her engaged. After the bath, you can also give your baby a massage. To do so, lay him or her on a towel, and rub some baby oil all over the back, stomach, hands, and legs. A massage after a bath will make your baby feel even more relaxed.

Once bath time is over, it will be time for bed. Take your baby to the bedroom and gently rock him or her, while snuggling. You can also sing a lullaby. When you see that your baby is becoming drowsy, put him or her down on the cot.

Allow your baby to slowly fall asleep on her own. Such a bedtime routine will help regulate your baby's sleep, and your baby will soon begin to understand what will happen after she is given a bath. This way not only will your baby relate to the pattern, but also be more relaxed as sudden transitions can lead to unnecessary excitement or alertness.

Sleep Cues

Now, as mentioned before, it is important to understand your baby's sleep cues. This will make establishing a bedtime routine much easier. Given below are several sleep cues that you can look out for.

- Another very common sleep cue for babies is rubbing the eyes. When sleep, your baby will start rubbing her eyes and might even start yawning, which in itself is a tell-tale sign.

- Other than rubbing eyes, your baby might also start scratching or rubbing the years and then move on to scratching her head as well. This is usually a sigh for sleep, especially if your baby stops doing anything else and concentrates on rubbing and scratching her ears. However, if your baby is doing this, then make sure to check for any infections as well.

- When your baby is very tired and sleepy, she will begin to whine or cry. This might start slowly and then grow into much louder cries. If you see this is happening, then immediately try to soothe your baby, before she becomes any more frantic.

- Sometimes when sleepy, your baby might make small

grunting noises. Now, this might be difficult for you to understand, because babies often make such noises while playing or when trying to mimic the adults. This is your baby's way of communicating as she is not able to talk. So, pay attention to what your baby is doing when she is making these noises and look for any of the other cues as well.

- Your baby will also become quite clingy when sleepy and will start protesting when you try to settle him or her down. At times like this, rock your baby and cuddle till she is quite drowsy. Then you can gently lay him or her down on the cot.

Eleven Tips to Help Parents Sleep Better

New parents often find it difficult to get proper sleep, and this sleep deprivation can last for a couple of months. However, getting proper rest is of the utmost importance because caring for your baby in a sleep-deprived state can be quite dangerous.

Most of the time, you will find that you are too exhausted to complete all chores. For example, if you have not had a good night's sleep in a while, and you are driving your baby to the pediatrician, it is extremely dangerous and can lead to accidents if you doze off behind the wheel.

Also, lack of sleep is found to increase several postpartum mood problems in new mothers. But while understanding the hazards of sleep deprivations, new parents still struggle to strike a balance, and usually, they are unable to take time off and allow themselves to catch a break and rest.

Given below are eleven tips that can help you to take rest, even when you need to remain completely alert for your baby.

- Before you have your baby, understand that you will probably be sleep deprived in a few weeks and discuss this with your partner. The two of you can figure out how you want to deal with and even discuss if you would like a night nurse after a few months (once the baby is a little older). It is important to understand your sleep needs and decide on how you want to take care of them.

- During the time that you are in the hospital, let your baby sleep in the hospital nursery. Hospital nurseries have nurses who are trained and will give good care to your baby. After giving birth, you will need to rest yourself, and this is the best way to do it. This will just be for one or two nights, but even that bit of rest can go a long way in keeping you healthy.

- Do not take up any added responsibilities once you have your baby. With a new-born, your hands are going to be full. So whenever you do get a little time (when your baby is sleeping without fussing), take some rest. Do not fill that time up with extra errands. If you are a young mother with an older child at home, ask your partner to take her to school and attend games or school meetings.

- The best way for new parents to get rid of sleep deprivation is to sleep when the baby is sleeping. Once your baby falls asleep, stop whatever you are doing and get some rest yourself. You might want to finish off chores, do laundry or do the dishes, once you find some time, or make some calls. However, your work can wait as you need to take care of yourself first if you want to be able to attend to your baby properly.

- Always accept help from other family members and friends during this time. Sleep is a basic necessity, so allow a close family member or friend to step in and help for some time while you take a break and sleep. You can also engage a babysitter if you wish to. There is nothing wrong with taking some time off as it is a medical requirement. Therefore, do not hesitate to accept any help that you can get, and then once you do have someone to attend to your baby, try getting some sleep.

- New parents are often concerned about the fact that if they fall asleep, they will not be able to hear their baby crying. When babies wake up crying, it actually works as a natural alarm clock, so there is really no need to worry. The only way you will not be able to hear your baby is if the nursery is quite far from your bedroom. In the case, you can always have a baby monitor installed.

- It is important to divide the tasks among yourselves. If you are a new mother who is breastfeeding her baby, consider pumping some milk into a bottle so that your partner can give it to your baby during the night-time feeding sessions. Also try outsourcing the household abilities, because you will be exhausted to do them on your own.

- It is important for parents to understand that while babies can initially be fussy, they will also start sleeping through the night once they are a few months older. However, this also means that you should catch on some sleep whenever you can. Do not give on having a full night's sleep as once your baby is sleeping throughout a whole night, you will too.

- Loss of sleep can often lead to mood swings. If you are sleep deprived, you are likely to be depressed, and you will feel like not doing anything. Do not ignore this feeling, but actively try to let it go. Too much sleep loss can lead to postpartum depression, so if you will like your mood swings are getting quite frequent, and you are able to identify a few symptoms, consult your doctor immediately. In the meanwhile take as much rest as possible.

- Short naps can help a lot. Therefore, get as many of those as possible. Even if what you need is a few hours of sleep, about forty-five minutes of naptime will actually make you feel more energetic than you were feeling before.

- Do not share your bed with your baby. New parents often want to hold their baby close and cuddle them while sleeping. But bedsharing will only make you more alert. If you place your baby in a cot and sleep alone in your bed, you will get better sleep, as you will not constantly be worrying about her.

Conclusion

This brings us to the end of this guide. Undoubtedly, training your kid to sleep throughout the nice could be a tough task, to begin with. However, with proper steps, you can take care of this aspect fairly well.

In this guide, we discussed the importance of proper sleep, and we also focused on various ways through which you can ensure that your baby enjoys a night's sleep peacefully.

Happy parenting!

9 781951 643034